فى المَطالِعِ التَّنجيم

The
FORTUNES
of
ASTROLOGY

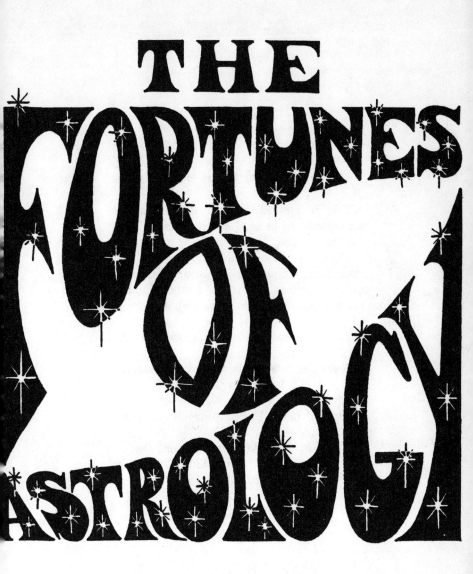

THE FORTUNES OF ASTROLOGY

A new, complete treatment
of the Arabic Parts

Robert Hurzt Granite

International Standard Book Number 0-917086-27-9

Cover design and chapter heading sketches
by Robert Hurzt Granite

Printed in the United States of America

Published by ACS Publications, Inc.
P.O. Box 16430
San Diego, CA 92116-0430

First Printing, July 1981
Second Printing, February 1985

DEDICATION

The one person who is most responsible for my study of astrology; the person who does my charts for me; the person who argues most with me; and the person who encourages me the most, is my mother, Della Snyder Bliss, to whom I dedicate this book with all my love and appreciation for her constant influences.

I give special thanks to all who have influenced my particular curiosities and researches along the side branches of astrology; Margaret Latvala, Mayne Kenney, Ivy M.G. Jacobson (who also graciously proofread this manuscript and vastly improved it for me). Lila Gregory, Gene Lockhart, Roberta Wilson, Karma Welch, Ramona Hogan, Annette Carter, my editor Cherie Jameison, my publisher Neil Michelsen and the beautiful lady who guided my first steps on the road of astrological interpretation, Flaucy Schwenk.

CONTENTS

Foreword ix

I   Whence Come the Fortunes? 1

II   What are We Reading? 5

III   The Lists 15

IV   The Methods 39

V   Fortunes in the Houses 61

VI   Fortunes in the Signs 93

VII   Fortuna in Wreck-tification 103

FOREWORD

During the 1960's astrology enjoyed a great resurgence. The 1970's brought us astrological buzz-words as the "in" type of cocktail conversation, but a decline in sincere interest. Now we are at the beginning of the new decade of the 1980's. The question seems to be "What's going to happen now to astrology?" I think we can see where astrology is going by looking at where it's been.

Sometime before 4,000 B.C. Aryan hordes swooped down from the north, with their male deities, to obliterate just about all records of the goddess-worshipping Mediterraneans and Indians. In those days astrology was already a very complex science. With the imposition of the male deity over the female deity, most of the old texts were rewritten. All the hermaphrodite qualities of astrology were cast into strictly male or female qualities, to suit the more simplistic northerners. What was changed must remain conjecture, as they were very thorough in their forced conversion. However, logic and some of the remaining records of Sumer and the traditions of India tell us that astrology must have originally concerned itself with the fixed stars and the constellations. They were the most dependable things in man's world of constant change. There is enough evidence in elk horn and stone scratchings to tell us that it was the northern Aryans who were so change-oriented, that they focused only on the planets.

As a working hypothesis, let us accept the idea that man did not *see pictures in the night skies* and then circumscribe the constellations according to his artistic vision. Let us understand that man noted that people who were born when certain groupings of stars were on the apparent rising or setting horizons or directly overhead, exhibited certain characteristics in common. These characteristics *seemed* animalistic, bird-like, aquatic, heroic or ultra-humanistic. Once this correlation was made, the symbolic mind of man assigned the *shape* to that grouping of stars, for easy reference. Some of these shapes were very earthly and human, some were extremely creative fantasies but each shape *(constellation)* represented symbolically what man had observed as the *effects* of that group of stars, when manifested in the life of a person.

Man *did not* see pictures in the night sky first and look for effects later. He saw the demonstrated effects and then symbolically *assigned* the shapes, so his all too simple mind could keep track of the knowledge that was literally overflowing his cranial capacities. Man simplified into symbolism that which was beyond his abilities to correlate — demonstrations of truth too vast for him to encompass. To save his own sanity and allow him to continue working in the society of his day, man created or found the symbolism which did correlate to the observed effect. In that respect mankind has not changed a bit throughout the ages. We are still trying to simplify the staggering, by forcing into acceptable symbolism, those things which are beyond our comprehension. In this way we kid ourselves that we have "mastered" the incomprehensible.

Many astrological groups are trying to *pare* astrology down to only those points which are *fail-proof*. This usually indicates being insecure or uninformed. I do not disapprove because I know what these scientific researches must eventually lead them into the mind boggling mystery schools, which in their initial "clean-cut," limiting precepts, are what they are trying to get away from. However, I do lament the time they are spending, trying to limit the world's oldest science to only perceivable, mundane characteristics, psychological nuances, character inhibiters and so forth without end. Each person to *their* own vision. Each of these people exhibit a dogmatic superiority, with which they try to discredit anything that falls outside of their own *supreme vision*. I would like to see them spending all of that time rediscovering the validity of the spade work done for us by the centuries of mankind which preceded us. Those were people of truly scientific inquisitiveness and some, even of vision, whose objectives were to expand the precepts of themselves, mankind and the universe, of which they were most obviously a part. They did not try to limit the whole of universal knowledge to kindergarten character analysis.

At the present time astrology seems to be standing still. Little groups are pairing off and stamping their feet petulantly and saying, in effect, "I won't go any further until *you* prove this or that to *me*." I'm sorry but the burden of proof is always on the shoulders of the questioner. If you can't prove it to your own satisfaction, ignore it. Maybe later on you will be mature enough to discover it. In the meantime, don't downgrade those who are trying to prove it to *their* satisfaction.

This book grew out of a challenge just that simple. I discovered Arabic parts when studying primary delineation. Then I ignored them because they didn't always read true. Next, I was amazed when I discovered how long they had been around. The ancient Assyrians used them, Ptolemy, Kepler and Isaac Newton used them and today, Charles A. Jayne, Ivy Jacobson and Phyllis D. Harrison use them. So I said to myself, "There's got to be *something* there." That started my research project, never dreaming that it would become a book. I know in advance that there are astrologers who will read this work and say, "Well, if you can't get all of your answers from the planets, you're no astrologer." Others will call these extra tools (which the Fortunes are) interesting playthings.

I feel that astrology is now at a plateau of regrouping itself. I feel that this plateau is only temporary — a pause to retest our foundations before we soar a little further beyond the considerations of that physical-material world which *appears* to mark our limitations. All the little noises we hear of placing "scientific" limitations on astrology are merely ways of testing astrology's validity. When, once again, astrology breaks through scientific limitations, it will expand science itself. As in ages past, astrology is headed toward encompassing the incomprehensible in symbolism which does not limit astrology's application. This means that we must make allowances for *freak* phenomena within the framework of the familiar symbolism. We cannot afford to discard a precept just because one, ten or a hundred instances *seem* to refute the accepted delineation. The accepted delineations must be expanded, not limited, to make room for the freaks. These freaks are merely manifestations indicating that we don't know all there is to know — yet.

Many modern astrologers have lost track of the fact that astrology, like all other sciences, is an observational process. The limits apparent in astrology are only the limits that individuals bring with them when they become astrologers: *the ability to observe*, and/or *what they choose to observe*.

Materialist astrologers will perceive only solid phenomena; so they will limit astrology to the stock market, race track, investment counseling and the like. Humanistic astrological counselors will focus only on the interplay of the five senses and the psychological levels of compatibilities of people in partnerships. Occult astrologers will find the "cycles of great forces," which they can bend to their magics. Spiritual astrologers look only at the tools which tell them how they and their clients can make this "veil of tears" more comprehensible. Mystic astrologers play with the motivative skeins of free-will and destiny, with which they hope to control (or at least direct) all the influences of life.

These are all various manifestations of the "scientific" astrologer, in that they only look at the things they are looking for. A complete astrologer tries to encompass all of these levels, and searches for more. Such astrologers have a marvelous trick of approaching each chart with a childlike wonder, instead of trying to consciously focus. In this way they leave themselves open to the process of discovery. After their wondering has discovered, *then* they focus, to bring it into consciousness so they can track it down. The differences here are simply that one group uses the scientific *process*. The other groups uses scientific *curiosity*, which I have called — wondering, *then* applies the scientific process.

I lay no claim to being a complete astrologer. However, this book grew out of such a process as I have outlined. If this type of adventure appeals to you, follow it through *The Fortunes of Astrology*.

Robert Hurzt Granite
Los Angeles, Calif.
September 15, 1980

Chapter I
WHENCE COME
THE FORTUNES

This book is not designed to be the last on the *Fortunes*, commonly called *Arabic parts or points*: This book is designed to be a limited guidebook — the limitations being of my own research, experience and observations. Hopefully it will open to you a new perspective on this side branch of astrology, a side branch touted by the ancient astrologers but heretofore unreliable in our modern computations.

The Fortunes are not a short-cut to every astrological problem. They are not an easy method to make a beginner look like a professional. The Fortunes are an aid and a tool which, properly used, can be of the utmost value when you are hit by an out-of-left-field question during the interpretation of an astrological chart.

Arabic parts are not Arabic, so I will call them what the Ancients and the Arabs called them, **The Fortunes**. It was the Arabic astrologer, Al-Biruni, who in his book *The Elements of Astrology* gave the most exhaustive list of the Fortunes. He collected them from all over the then-known world, from past civilizations and even from some mysterious people he refers to as the Ancients. Al-Biruni is to be considered the foremost authority on the subject. Because he was Arabic, Westerners began calling this compilation Arabic Parts. Al-Biruni's book was compiled and written in 1029 A.D.; to my knowledge his information on the Fortunes has not been updated until now.

Just what are the Fortunes, who discovered them and/or

when were they first used? As with many other things dating before
the dawn of modern history, the records are either missing or were
destroyed by the zeal of some religious sect who gained control from
time to time, in the hope of making everything dependent upon its
guru, teacher or saviour. Like all other valid practices in astrology,
the Fortunes could not have been invented. They had to be
discovered by observation or, as the mystics say it, by "spiritual
memory."

We can only imagine the incident leading to the discovery of
the Fortunes. Picture, if you will, the consternation of one of the
"Ancients" when it was observed that events were happening in his
life which were not triggered or forecast by planets, cusps, fixed
stars, solstice and/or midpoints. This ancient one already knew that
by astrology everything in the universe could be timed and
measured. He knew that astrology held the sum total of mankind's
efforts to read and understand all the laws of Nature and of God.
This ancient was not superstitious nor was he an intellectual sloth.
He understood that the limit of his understanding was within his
own mind. This true adept was not about to dismiss the event with
the over-used phrase: "It's the will or the caprice of (the) God(s)."

He began studying what he knew—the event and his astrological tools.

For the sake of speculation, let us say that the event was one of
delightful surprise. The event was in harmony with his emotional
desires and his intellectual will, and it made his physical being tingle
with joy—a very fortunate event indeed. But he could see nothing in
his chart indicating that event! Let's assume that the event involved
his child. He could find the event in the child's chart; but being a
true initiate, he wanted to find it in *his* chart. He knew he could not
compute charts for each and every person known by or related to
those who would seek out his services.

In his chart the fifth house or division was empty. He was
aware that on the day of the event both the Sun and Jupiter were
throwing trines to almost the same degree of that empty fifth
division. Years of research must have gone into the working out of
why that untenanted point in the fifth division of his chart elicited
such a strong impact. Once alerted, he discovered that adverse
aspects to this blank degree seemed to work also. With the passing
of time more and more evidence piled up, without a nail to hang it
on.

Accidentally (or was it spiritual memory?) while playing with various other charts, he lightly tossed a solar equilibrium chart over his own natal chart. Excitedly he grabbed them and held them up to the Sun. His Moon, in the solar equilibrium chart *fell in his empty fifth division!* Frantically he began figuring out *just what degree* in his natal chart would hold this spector of the Moon. Lo! it was the exact degree that had been receiving those beautiful trines on the day of the fortunate event which involved his child!

How happy our Ancient must have been, to be able to present to his fellow-adepts this newly-discovered, previously hidden relationship between the Sun, Moon and Ascendant ON A THREE-DIMENSIONAL LEVEL!...and how bewildered he must have been when they laughed at him, thinking that he had invented it. Our unknown ancient most likely died a sour and embittered man. Or did he realize that on the day of his presentation, Saturn was conjunct his fortunate point?

The other adepts never stopped laughing at Old So-and-so...never...until something that was not signified in the chart happened to them or one of their loved ones.

Let's say the event was a death for which no usual astrological significators could be found. Death as noted astrologically, involves three things, three being the mystic number of creation and the *root* of the number of completion: 1) the physical body (that brings in the Ascendant again); 2) the eighth division or house (another cusp); 3) the Moon, that giver of life, being absent. "MY GOD!" that second ancient one might have screamed, "It works. It works!", as he discovered Saturn was in malefic opposition to the degree the eighth cusp would hit if the lunar equilibrium chart were placed over the natal chart.

In all intellectual and empirical research, the criteria is as simple as that...IT WORKS. Understanding comes later. Refinement follows but first we must find out that it works. For example, who is to say that they truly understand what electricity is; but it works and so we use it.

By 1029 A.D. we find the Fortunes to be a long list. Different astrologers used different planets, cusps and points to figure the same Fortune or Misfortune.

Al-Biruni faithfully listed all the variations known to him; by his time the formula has been set. As Al-Biruni wrote: "All Fortunes involve the beginning of the matter, the end of the matter and the casting off point or catalyst."

With this understanding, any astrologer well versed in the laws of natural and/or supernatural phenomena, and knowing the full meaning of the astrological symbols, is free to discover new Fortunes. Like everyone else, astrologers are limited only by their ability to perceive.

For example, The Part of Fortune — the beginning of the matter starts with a personal involvement (the Ascendant). If you're looking for Fortuna in achievement or spirituality, perhaps you could use the Midheaven or the twelfth house cusp. The end of the matter usually involves an emotional victory or exaltation. So, to the Ascendant we "add" the Moon. To complete this triad, we must cast off or cut out something. The one thing that stands in most people's way of receiving benefits is their own will, which tries to force things to fall into a pattern that they can understand. So we "subtract" the Sun to get rid of that.

For the Point of Death we "add" the eighth cusp of death *and* regeneration to the physical body of the Ascendant. Then we "subtract" the Moon, that giver and protector of life. So it is with all the Fortunes: 1)The beginning of the question; 2)the end of the question; and 3)the casting off point, being the celestial body that interferes with the completion. It's like the knitted shawl of life, creation or the universe.

Chapter II
WHAT ARE WE READING?

The purpose of this chapter is to give you *my* understanding of a few of the Fortunes from Al-Biruni's lists. This is not meant to be a final word, but simply a guideline for you to form a foundation for your own interpretation. Hopefully it will be a wedge by which you begin to use the Fortunes. It is offered as a springboard for *you* to do your own research, offering clues and ideas of what you are looking at, so you'll know what you're looking for. Freely go beyond my simple understanding and make your own contribution to the vast library of astrological knowledge.

The Fortunes *are not planets*, so they cannot actively aspect anything. They are sensitive reaction points of varying magnitudes. As such they only receive aspects or influences from the following:

1. The natal planets and angles
2. The transiting planets
3. The directed or progressed planets and angles
4. A conjunction or opposition among themselves (squares, trines and sextiles do not seen to make much impact between the various Fortunes, but you may like to research this for yourself.)
5. From fixed stars. These fixed stars are of the utmost importance, because with a Fortune conjunct or opposing one of these influences, you may see them acting like a planet. It can *seem* to give aspects and not just be a negative receiver.

Since the Fortunes are not heavenly bodies but earthly reaction points, they have no declination, except earthly latitude and/or longitude. Therefore, we do not have to consider the declination of the fixed stars in relationship to the Fortunes. I have observed their "improper" and active behaviour even with Canopus, which is 75N50. Heavy aspects from one or more planets (natal, transit, direction or progression) can activate the Fortunes. The final touch off of a Fortune is usually by a strong transit which, depending on its quality (benefic, malefic, fiery, earthy, airy, watery, etc.), will set the keynote for its activation. When a Fortune is touched off, it will react in the person's life along the lines of the house position and the aspects the natal and progressed charts indicate. So there is no pat method of interpretation.

The following delineations are for reasonably bland aspected Fortunes when touched off by a benefic.

1. **FORTUNA:** As with all the Fortunes, much depends on the rest of the chart to tell you on what level the natives are functioning. In the chart of a materialistic, Fortuna means money. In the chart of an intellectual, it means knowledge and processed data. Specifically, it means *where the natives feel gain* and *what makes them feel fortunate*. Consider what house and Sign it is in and the aspects it is receiving. Apply all your know-how. The decanates and dwads will help you show how the fortunate feeling comes about. If it is receiving strong squares the natives will feel alive and fortunate when they are forced to make decisions along the lines indicated by their ambitions. Again, what house and sign are the squares coming from? Is it receiving many trines? The natives could feel fortunate only when indolent. If only one trine is present the fortunate feeling could manifest only when, after long and concentrated effort, the goal is achieved from some unexpected source where effort has not been expended. Now take the keywords for all the other aspects, houses and signs that are beaming in on Fortuna and apply them. This goes for all the Fortunes. The Fortunes are part of the art or creative side of astrology, so there are no pat formulas whereby you can state that such-and-such means this-and-that. This is what helps to make each chart individual and each individual unique. For the most part, astrology deals with individualities, not generalities. Perhaps this is why astrology will never be able to regulate itself to the compartmentalized generalities of accepted science. This is also the allure and adventurous challenge of astrology.

2. **DAEMON, RELIGION OR SPIRIT:** This indicates where, how and when the natives may unlock their personal perceptions of the non-apparent motivations of physical and material manifestations. This is the personal, non apparent foundation of the individual's faith and beliefs. This can be the measure of the progress of their soul's evolution.

3. **FRIENDSHIP AND LOVE:** Since this uses Fortuna and Spirit, it is obviously not physical or carnal friendship or love that is being indicated. This is rather those eternal qualities where the natives can find dependable understanding, no matter what they have done, plus that love that transcends the possessiveness of mundane love. The house it falls in tells from what quarter or department of life it will manifest. The degree will indicate a person whose Sun, Ascendant or major planetary influence will be on or near that degree. The nearer the degree, the more dependable the person will be. The aspects will tell how elated or depressed the natives will be before they are capable of searching out this type of love and friendship and what they will have to go through before they realize or experience it.

4. **DESPAIR, PENURY AND FRAUD:** Depending on the quarter of the chart where this part falls, this indicates whether the native traffics in these qualities or whether they are visited in the life from outside. The rest of your know-how will eventually be able to pinpoint the time they are most likely to happen.

5. **CAPTIVITY, PRISONS AND ESCAPE THEREFROM:** The first aspect by transit *and* direction to this point tell when captivity is likely to take place. The natal aspects tell how or under what circumstances it will happen. The second direction and transiting aspect tells when escape or release is likely to happen. Likewise, the natal aspects tell the conditions it will be accepted under. Depending on the house and sign placement, this could be captivity and imprisonment in a hospital, by love, by contract or greed. Remember that good aspects and benefic planets *fulfill* the promise. Bad aspects or malefic planets *deny* the promise. In this case, a conjunction, square or opposition of Saturn could cancel captivity. This would give the native time to reconsider alternative action or pile up more reasons and rationale why they can not avoid captivity, which a good aspect from Jupiter could fulfill.

6. **VICTORY, TRIUMPH AND AID:** As is true with all For-

tunes whose computation uses another Fortune, this part is more inclined to be of a personal, inner or spiritual nature. This Fortune
would undoubtedly involve material-social credits, especially if it
falls on an angle. It indicates one of those "ah ha!" or "eureka!"
incidents in life. Apply your knowledge and find out where, when,
why and how.

7. **VALOR AND BRAVERY:** This position tells where the
natives may gain merit or stand out above the crowd by their own
efforts (Mars) and inner resources (Fortuna). Very often they will
not be conscious of what is happening, because as in qualities at-
tributed to the asteroid Lulu, they may have some blinders that do
not allow them to see the muck on the road they are traveling until
they have passed it. The glint of gold is usually too strong for the
native to be concerned with creature comforts. So the mouse
becomes a lion and the coward a hero! It's in everyone's chart
somewhere, waiting to be uncovered.

8. **LIFE:** These next three Fortunes concern the first house, so
they are rather personal to the natives. Even though the formula
may be repeated later, it is related to another department of life
(house) so it will be read differently. The part of life is where the
natives have their hold on physical existence. It is their inherent
vitality and the degree of gusto with which they live. In spite of
other indicators to the contrary, this part can give you a clue as to
whether the natives, might die through illness or infirmity. Conversely, it can be an additional indication of an early death or a long
life.

9. **PILLAR OF THE HOROSCOPE, PERMANENCE, CON-
STANCE:** This indicates the spark or spirit beyond the physical
manifestation of the native. As with any Fortune, if badly placed,
heavily afflicted or debilitated by the lights, it can indicate a lack of
these qualities, if the natives are strongly based only in the physical.
If they are consciously trying to advance, even malignancies will only serve to drive them to perfecting and bringing into their consciousness these qualities. So you must be able to read the rest of the
chart too.

10. **REASONING AND ELOQUENCE, MIND:** This tells
where the natives, can apply their energies (Mars) to mental (Mercury) growth. The aspects tell how. The transits and directions tell
when.

11. **PROPERTY, GOODS:** These next three are related to the second house, because they relate to the use of the native's talents, abilities and possessions. The modern reading of money for this house is a sad indication of our current mental state. This Fortune indicates what the natives have as inherent qualities to get them by in this world. Much is dependent on the ruler or lord of the house, and the sign this Fortune falls in, whether these qualities are material, mental, emotional, spiritual or whatever. These are the native's strong points for success.

12. **DEBT:** This is where the natives pit their mental (Mercury) talents against the system (Saturn) in which they are living. If the natives are capable of seeing how to gain their ends while working within the system, debt may be avoided or they may be able to manipulate debts on a financier level. If not, the directions and transits will time it.

13. **TREASURE TROVE:** An ancient part not much used any more. If it is not completely destroyed by placement or aspects, it is an indicator of where the natives may combine their sense of values (Venus) with their mental aims (Mercury) to find the treasures in life that will make them more than simply content. These last three Fortunes bring home the fact that the Fortunes themselves are merely other facets for exercising selection and compromise necessary in the societies of the world.

14. **BROTHERS AND SISTERS:** These next three Fortunes concern the third house and have to do only with brothers and sisters. I suggest you try them as a method of reading the people's mental capabilities as well as the conditions they choose to "neighborhood" in. If siblings are indicated in the chart, this part will help to qualify the native's relationships (love, hate, friendship, distrust, tolerance, intolerance, dominance, submissiveness) with brothers and sisters. If debilitated to the point where brothers and sisters are lacking, read as mental abilities or neighborhoods.

15. **NUMBER OF BROTHERS AND SISTERS:** Being an only child, I have not worked with this one too much. But I suggest that its placement in the chart, where the third house may be empty and the ruler is not in a fertile or double-bodied sign, would be the indication of large families I have seen under these conditions.

16. **DEATH OF BROTHERS AND SISTERS:** Besides in-

dicating the method of death of these family members, the transits and directions mark these events clearly (other indicators willing). The placement of this part usually indicates the presence or lack of emotional impact that these deaths evoke in the native. Consider that this could also mean the time of death of mental dogmas the native has cherished or the death of the neighborhood the native chooses to live in.

FORTUNES 17 THROUGH 20 are almost a repeat of the last three, except they refer to parents and ancestry and belong to the fourth house.

21 & 22 REAL ESTATE: The two formulas themselves will tell you the two different types of real estate under consideration. In Hermes' Moon-Saturn formula we are obviously talking about land to live on and enough left over to expand our horizons. In the Persian Jupiter-Mercury formula we are obviously talking about investment lands or land to be exploited or improved to make a profit for the speculator. The aspects these Fortunes receive will pretty well delineate whether or not the native should invest in real estate. The placement by house and sign will indicate the best direction for the real estate development.

23 AGRICULTURE (Ancient) FORTUNE IN HUSBANDRY & MARRIAGE FOR WOMEN (Modern): Confused that one formula could be taken as an indication of such diversified categories? Either way, there's some plowing to be done. In ancient times, none thought of owning land or property until he was successfully married. During the Middle Ages, when all land was owned by a lord, people worked the land whether they were married or not. The Saturn-Venus Fortune was observed to be prominent when the man took a wife or when the woman took a husband. In ancient times the land was not given until the man had someone to help him plow or until the woman found some man whose field she would like or consent to plow. Briefly, the difference between the ancient agriculture and the modern fortune in husbandry is due to the society of the times.

I believe by now you have a pretty good idea of what the Fortunes are. I do not want to inflict my interpretation on you and I do not want to make this book into an encyclopedia. I only want to guide you to use your own common sense and astrological knowledge so that your know-how will grow along your own lines and not mine.

Any time you want to expand the Fortunes, try. For instance when someone asks about other people in their life, for whom you have no charts, look at the house cusp or planet that represents those other people. Turn the chart around as if that house or planet were the Ascendant. Now apply the formula from the lists of Fortunes that best fits the question. Suddenly you have a keyhole into an entirely new perspective.

If it is a lover who is being asked about, substitute the fifth house for the Ascendant. Immediately the second house becomes the Midheaven, the twelfth house becomes the eighth and so on. Without doing an extra chart you can see how the lover's activities are apt to affect the person you are counseling. This is what the querent really wants to know anyway. With this technique you are not reading the lover's chart. You are reading what effect the lover will have on the querent *from the querent's point of view*. The way the querent *thinks* the lover sees him or her is indicated by the querent's ninth house. The fifth house from the fifth house is the ninth house. Actually, the querent thinks that *only* the partner really knows him or her because the seventh house from the seventh house is the first house. This might be a clue to why people fall in love with their doctors and psychiatrists, who exhibit such understanding of them.

This may or may not be realistic, but it most certainly is the way the querents will see it, react to it and remember any event involving that person in their life.

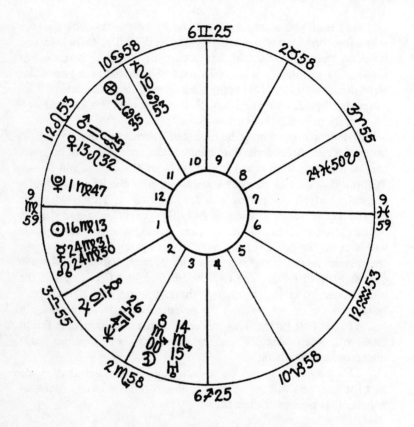

Abril-Rayhan Muhamman Ibn Ahmad Al-Biruni Tropical—Placidus

Born; September 4, 973 (Old Style)
Kath, Kwarizim (now Biruni, Uzbekistan)
60 E 10 - 41 N 33
5:05 A.M.
Source: Dr. J. K. Fotheringham
Chart computed by: Research Data, Inc.
917 So. Lombard Ave. - Oak Park, Ill. 60304

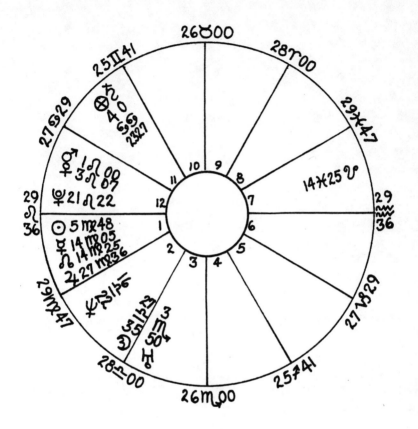

Abril-Rayhan Muhamman Ibn Ahmad Al-Biruni Sidereal — Campanus

Born; September 4, 973 (Old Style)
Kath, Kwarizim (now Biruni, Uzbekistan)
60 E 10 — 41 N 33
5:05 A.M.
Vernal Point 19:33:39
Source: Dr. J. K. Fortheringham
Chart computed by: Research Data, Inc.
917 So. Lombard Ave. - Oak Park, Ill. 60304

Chapter III
THE LISTS

First, I will list the Fortunes collected by Al-Biruni in his book *Elements of Astrology*. The original of this book now lies in the Victoria and Albert Museum in London, where only a few privileged people have access to it. Fortunately for the modern student, A.S.I. promises to bring out an inexpensive edition of this astrological treasure, making it available to all sincere students.

Where modern people have renamed the Fortunes of Al-Biruni's list, I will give the modern name in parenthesis, and the credit to the modern astrologer, if known to me.

Following this initial list will be a modern listing of those Fortunes developed since Al-Biruni's time. Again, where it is known, I will give personal or school credits. Many of the modern Fortunes were developed in the Hamburg School of Astrology, recognized as the Uranian astrology incubation ground. The Hamburg School chose the most relevant Fortunes (according to them) and renamed them trans-Neptunian planets, producing an astounding ephemeris of their transiting positions.*

The terms CHANGE and DON'T CHANGE used throughout the lists refer to births between sunset and sunrise (night births). This simply means to reverse the formula. Add what the formula says to subtract and subtract what the formula says to add. A night

*Calvin Hanes, in informal discussion Summer 1972 at First Temple of Astrology, Los Angeles, California.

birth is easy to identify. If the Sun is *below* the horizon line or the north half of the chart, it is a night birth. If the Sun is above the horizon line, or the south half of the chart, it is a day birth and you will not change the formula. With these few words I now present to you the lists, both ancient and modern.

AL-BIRUNI'S LIST OF FORTUNES

PART OF	FORMULA	FOR NIGHT BIRTHS
1 Fortune (Fortuna)	Asc. + Moon − Sun	Change
2 Daemon, Religion, Spirit	Asc. + Sun − Moon	Change
3 Friendship & Love	Asc. + Spirit − Fortune	Change
4 Despair, Penury & Fraud	Asc. + Fortuna − Spirit	Change
5 Captivity, Prisons & Escape therefrom	Asc. + Fortuna − Saturn	Change
6 Victory, Triumph & Aid	Asc. + Jupiter − Spirit	Change
7 Valor & Bravery	Asc. + Fortuna − Mars	Change

FORTUNES OF THE TWELVE HOUSES

FIRST HOUSE

8 Life (Reincarnation- P. Grell)	Asc. + Saturn − Jupiter	Change
9 Pillar of the Horoscope, Permanence, Constance	Asc. + Spirit − Fortuna	Change
10 Reasoning & Eloquence (Mind- modern)	Asc. + Mars − Mercury	Change

SECOND HOUSE

11 Property & Goods	Asc. + Second Cusp − Lord of Second Cusp	Change
12 Debt	Asc. + Mercury − Saturn	Change
13 Treasure Trove	Asc. + Venus − Mercury	Don't Change

THIRD HOUSE

14 Brothers & Sisters (Family- M.E. Jones)	Asc. + Jupiter − Saturn	Don't Change
15 Number of Brothers & Sisters	Asc. + Saturn − Mercury	Don't Change
16 Death of Brothers & Sisters	Asc. + 10° of 3rd − Sun	Change

continued

PART OF	FORMULA	FOR NIGHT BIRTHS
FOURTH HOUSE		
17 Parents (Father-modern)	Asc. + Saturn − Sun (some − Jupiter)	Change
18 Death of Parents	Asc. + Jupiter − Saturn	Change
19 Grandparents	Asc. + Saturn − 2nd Cusp.	Change
20 Ancestors & Relations	Asc. + Mars − Saturn	Change
21 Real Estate (Hermes)	Asc. + Moon − Saturn	Change
22 Real Estate (Persian)	Asc. + Jupiter − Mercury	Change
23 Agriculture (Fortune in Husbandry & Marriage of Women - Modern)	Asc. + Saturn − Venus	Don't Change
24 Issue of Affairs	Asc. + Lord of New or Full Moon Prior to Birth − Saturn	Don't Change
FIFTH HOUSE		
25 Children	Asc. + Saturn − Jupiter	Change
26 Time, Number & Sexes of Children	Asc. + Jupiter − Mars	Don't Change
27 Condition of Males	Asc. + Jupiter − Mars	Don't Change
28 Condition of Females (Comfort — M.E. Jones)	Asc. + Venus − Moon	Don't Change
29 Expected Birth (M. or F.)	Asc. + Lord of Moon's House − Moon	Don't Change
SIXTH HOUSE		
30 Disease, Defects & Time of Onset (Hermes)	Asc. + Mars − Saturn	Don't Change
31 Disease, Defects & Time of Onset (Ancients)	Asc. + Mars − Mercury	Don't Change
32 Captivity	Asc. + Lord of Saturn's House − Saturn	Don't Change
33 Slaves (Servants—modern)	Asc. + Moon − Mercury	Don't Change

continued

PART OF	FORMULA	FOR NIGHT BIRTHS
SEVENTH HOUSE		
34 Marriage of Men Hermes)	Asc. + Venus − Saturn	Don't Change
35 Marriage of Men (Walis) (Contentment, Peace — modern) (Love & Entertainment—Ivy M.G. Jacobson)	Asc. + Venus − Sun	Don't Change
36 Trickery & Deception of Men and Women	Asc. + Venus − Sun	Don't Change
37 Intercourse (Verbal, Trade and??—for female?)	Asc. + Venus − Sun	Don't Change
38 Marriage of Women (Hermes)	Asc. + Saturn − Venus	Don't Change
39 Marriage of Women (Valens)	Asc. + Mars − Moon	Don't Change
40 Misconduct by Women	Asc. + Mars − Moon	Don't Change
41 Trickery & Deceit of Men by Women	Asc. + Mars − Moon	Don't Change
42 Intercourse (Verbal, Trade and??—for male?)	Asc. + Mars − Moon	Don't Change
43 Unchastity of Women	Asc. + Mars − Moon	Don't Change
44 Chastity of Women	Asc. + Venus − Moon	Don't Change
45 Marriage of Men & Women (Hermes) (Partners—modern)	Asc. + 7th Cusp − Venus	Don't Change
46 Time of Marriage (Hermes)	Asc. + Moon − Sun	Don't Change

continued

PART OF	FORMULA	FOR NIGHT BIRTHS
47 Fraudulent Marriage & Conditions Facilitating it	Asc. + Venus − Saturn	Don't Change
48 Sons-in-Law	Asc. + Venus − Saturn	Change
49 Lawsuits, Discord & Controversy (Waste & Extravagance — Ivy M. G. Jacobson)	Asc. + Jupiter − Mars	Change

EIGHTH HOUSE

50 Death	Asc. + 8th Cusp − Moon	Don't Change
51 Anareta (Taker of Life)	Asc. + Moon − Lord of Asc.	Change
52 Year to be feared for Death or Famine	Asc. + Lord of New or Full Moon Previous to Birth − Saturn	Don't Change
53 Place of Murder & Sickness	Asc. + Mars − Saturn	Change
54 Danger & Violence	Asc. + Mercury − Saturn	Change

NINTH HOUSE

55 Journeys	Asc. + 9th Cusp − Lord of 9th	Don't Change
56 Journeys by Water	Asc. + 15° Cancer − Saturn	Change
57 Timidity & Hiding (Travel, Faith, Trust & Belief—modern) (Prejudice—M.E. Jones)	Asc. + Mercury − Moon	Change
58 Deep Reflection	Asc. + Moon − Saturn	Change
59 Understanding & Wisdom	Asc. + Sun − Saturn	Change
60 Traditions & Knowledge of affairs (Fame, Recognition & Increase—modern)	Asc. + Jupiter − Sun	Change

continued

PART OF	FORMULA	FOR NIGHT BIRTHS
61 Knowledge, Whether True or False (Discernment & Education—modern) (Curiosity—M.E. Jones)	Asc. + Moon − Mercury	Don't Change
TENTH HOUSE		
62 Noble Births	Distance from Saturn (Lord of Time) to 21° Libra (Saturn's Exaltation)	Change
63 Kings (Rulers)	Asc. + Moon − Mars	Change
64 Administrators	Asc. + Mars − Mercury	Change
65 Ruler's Victory, Conquest (Fate, Fatality, Karma, Love of Brethern—modern)	Asc. + Saturn − Sun (if Saturn be combust, use Jupiter)	Change
66 Those Who Rise in Station (Sudden Advancement—modern)	Asc. + Fortuna − Saturn	Change
67 Celebrity of Rank	Asc. + Sun − Saturn	Don't Change
68 Armies & Police (Surgery & Accident—modern)	Asc. + Saturn − Mars	Change
69 Ruler: Those concerned in Nativities	Asc. + Moon − Saturn	Don't Change
70 Merchants & Their Work	Asc. + Venus − Mercury	Change
71 Buying & Selling Merchandise	Asc. + Fortuna − Spirit (Some − Moon)	Change
72 Operations & Orders in Medical Treatment	Asc. + Jupiter − Sun	Change
73 Mothers	Asc. + Moon − Venus	Change
ELEVENTH HOUSE		
74 Glory	Asc. + Spirit − Fortuna	Change
75 Friendship & Enmity	Asc. + Spirit − Fortuna	Change

continued

PART OF	FORMULA	FOR NIGHT BIRTHS
76 Revered by Man, Constant in Affairs & Honorable Acquaintances	Asc. + Sun − Fortuna	Change
77 Success	Asc. + Jupiter − Fortuna	Change
78 Worldliness	Asc. + Venus − Fortuna	Change
79 Hope (Integrity— M.E. Jones)	Asc. + Mercury − Jupiter	Change
80 Friends	Asc. + Mercury − Moon	Don't Change
81 Violence	Asc. + Mercury − Spirit	Don't Change
82 Abundance in House	Asc. + Sun − Moon	Don't Change
83 Liberty of Person	Asc. + Sun − Mercury	Change
84 Praise & Acceptance	Asc. + Venus − Jupiter	Change

TWELFTH HOUSE

85 Enmity (some Ancients)	Asc. + Mars − Saturn	Don't Change
86 Enmity (Hermes)	Asc. + 12th Cusp − Lord of 12th	Don't Change
87 Bad Luck	Asc. + Fortuna − Spirit	Don't Change

continued

FORTUNES NOT RELATED TO PLANETS OR HOUSES

PART OF	FORMULA	FOR NIGHT BIRTHS
88 Hailaj (Excitement of Transportation as in elevation)	Asc. + Moon − New or Full Moon Prior to Chart	Don't Change
89 Debilitated Bodies	Asc. + Mars − Fortuna	Change
90 Horsemanship, Bravery	Asc. + Moon − Saturn	Change
91 Boldness, Violence & Murder	Asc. + Moon − Lord of Asc.	Change
92 Trickery & Deceit	Asc. + Spirit − Mercury	Change
93 Necessity & Wish	Asc. + Mars − Saturn	Don't Change
94 Requirements & Necessities (Egyptians)	Asc. + 3rd Cusp − Mars	Don't Change
95 Realization of Needs & Desires	Asc. + Mercury − Fortuna	Don't Change
96 Retribution	Asc. + Sun − Mars	Change
97 Rectitude	Asc. + Mars − Mercury	Change

continued

FORTUNES FOR SPECIAL CHARTS

MUNDANE FORTUNES — FOR VERNAL EQUINOX AND NEW MOON CHARTS

PART OF	FORMULA	FOR NIGHT BIRTHS
1 Ruler's Lot	Jupiter + Prog. M.C. − Prog. Sun	Don't Change
2 By Another Way	Asc. + Prior New Moon − New Moon's Asc.	Don't Change
3 Victory (Falh Cultivation)	Asc. + Lord of 7th (some use 7th) − Sun	Don't Change
4 Battle	Victory + Moon − Mars	Don't Change
5 Battle (Umar)	Asc. + Moon − Mars	Don't Change
6 Battle (Al-Furkhan)	Asc. + Moon − Saturn	Don't Change
7 Truce between Armies	Asc. + Mercury − Moon	Don't Change
8 Conquest	Asc. + Mars − Sun	Don't Change
9 Triumph	Asc. + Jupiter − Fortuna	Change
10 First New Moon	Asc. + New Moon − Asc. of New Moon Year	Don't Change
11 Second New Moon	Asc. + New Moon − Asc. of New Moon	Don't Change

* * * * * *

FORTUNES ASSOCIATED WITH EQUINOX, SOLSTICE, NEW & FULL MOON CHARTS

PART OF	FORMULA	FOR NIGHT BIRTHS
1 Earth	Asc. + Jupiter − Saturn	Don't Change
2 Water	Asc. + Venus − Moon	Don't Change
3 Air & Wind	Asc. + Lord of 4th − Mercury	Don't Change
4 Fire	Asc. + Mars − Sun	Don't Change
5 Clouds	Asc. + Saturn − Mars	Change
6 Rains	Asc. + Venus − Moon	Change
7 Cold	Asc. + Saturn − Mercury	Change
8 Floods	Asc. + Saturn − Sun	Change at Moonrise instead of Sunset

* * * * *

FORTUNES FOR CROP PROGNOSTICATION
(COMMODITIES MARKET)

PART OF	FORMULA	FOR NIGHT BIRTHS
1 Wheat	Asc. + Jupiter − Sun	Change
2 Barley & Meats	Asc. + Jupiter − Moon	Change
3 Rice & Millet	Asc. + Venus − Jupiter	Change
4 Corn	Asc. + Saturn − Jupiter	Change
5 Pulse (Legumes)	Asc. + Mercury − Venus	Change
6 Lentils & Iron	Asc. + Saturn − Mars	Change
7 Beans, Onions	Asc. + Mars − Saturn	Change
8 Chick Peas	Asc. + Sun − Mercury	Change
9 Sesame, Grapes	Asc. + Venus − Saturn	Change
10 Sugar	Asc. + Mercury − Venus	Change
11 Honey	Asc. + Sun − Moon	Change
12 Oils	Asc. + Moon − Mars	Change
13 Nuts & Flax	Asc. + Venus − Mars	Change
14 Olives	Asc. + Moon − Mercury	Change
15 Apricots & Peaches	Asc. + Mars − Saturn	Change
16 Melons	Asc. + Mercury − Jupiter	Change
17 Salt	Asc. + Mars − Moon	Change
18 Sweets	Asc. + Mercury − Sun	Change
19 Astrigents	Asc. + Saturn − Mercury	Change
20 Pungent things	Asc. + Saturn − Mars	Change
21 Raw Silk, Cotton	Asc. + Venus − Mercury	Change
22 Purgatives	Asc. + Saturn − Mercury	Change
23 Bitter Purgatives	Asc. + Mars − Saturn	Change
24 Acid Purgatives	Asc. + Jupiter − Saturn	Change

* * * * *

FORTUNES FOR HORARY QUESTIONS

PART OF	FORMULA	FOR NIGHT BIRTHS
1 Secrets	Asc. + M.C. − Lord of the Ascendant	Don't Change
2 Urgent Wish	Asc. + Lord of Asc. − Lord of the Hour	Change
3 Time of Attainment	Asc. + Lord of M.C. − Lord of the Hour	Change
4 Information: True or False	Asc. + Moon − Mercury	Change
5 Injury to Business	Asc. + Fortuna − Lord of the Ascendant	Don't Change
6 Freedmen & Servants	Mercury + Saturn − Jupiter	Don't Change
7 Lords & Masters (Employers)	Moon + Saturn − Jupiter	Don't Change
8 Marriage	Asc. + 7th Cusp − Venus	Don't Change
9 Time for Action (Walis)	Asc. + Jupiter − Sun	Don't Change
10 Time Occupied in Action	Asc. + Saturn − Sun	Don't Change
11 Dismissal or Resignation	Saturn + Jupiter − Sun	Don't Change
12 Time of Resignation	M.C. + Fortuna − Lord of the Affair	Don't Change
13 Life or Death of Absent Person	Asc. + Mars − Moon	Don't Change
14 Lost Animal*	Asc. + Mars − Sun	Don't Change
15 Law Suit	Asc. + Mercury − Mars	Don't Change
16 Successful Issue	Asc. + Jupiter − Sun	Don't Change
17 Decapitation	8th Cusp + Mars − Moon	Don't Change
18 Torture	M.C. + Saturn − Moon	Don't Change

(*dark/black animal signified by Saturn; light animal by the Sun)

These are the Fortunes as collected by Al-Biruni. The growth of the use of the Fortunes did not end there. Throughout the world astrologers are discovering more Fortunes (reaction points) as they pursue their various fields of endeavor. Some of these Fortunes take no calculation, such as the following parts:

1 Earth-
is in the same degree but the opposite sign of the Sun. This Fortune tells the place where the natives put down their roots, the stand they take and much about their personal perspectives.

2 Illumination-
is the same degree but the opposite sign of Fortuna. It marks the area of non-sensory knowledge and inspiration.

3 Self (Rudhyar)-
is the Ascendant itself (yourself). Using this term brings to light many often overlooked facets of understanding, as the Ascendant *is the perspective* from which you view the rest of the world.

Other Fortunes take calculation; but use no cusps or planets, such as the part of:

4 Life-
Is advanced at the rate of 4°: 17':09'' per year, which takes it through a sign in seven years like a counterpoint to the Uranus cycle. It reads off in the chart like a steamroller type of progression. The confusion and arguement over it is, "Where do you start it?" Some start it at 0° of Aries from the moment of birth. Others start it with the degree, minute and second of the natal Sun. Still others use the

Ascendant. I might suggest some still different results could be obtained by using the Part of Life, Number 8 from Al-Biruni's lists.

In Pandit Gopesh Kumar Ojha's *One Thousand Aphorisms of Love and Marriage* will be found many oddball Fortunes that are designed to accurately time marital happiness and unhappiness.

1 Time of Prospects of
  Marriage-   Lord of the 1st + Lord of the 7th. When Jupiter conjuncts or trines this point, if it is well aspected natally, brings happiness. If not well aspected natally, it brings unhappiness.

2 Time of Fruition of
  Marriage or Partnership-   Lord of the 1st + Lord of the 7th + Venus. For good results, this is to be touched off by Jupiter.

3 Choice of Marriage
  Partner-   Lord of 1st + Venus. If conjunct or trine natal Moon, brings good choice of partnership. If in bad or trying aspect to natal Moon, brings trials as indicated (also apply these relationships to #1).

4 Conjugal Happiness-   Lord of 1st + Venus. If aspected by benefics, bodes well, if by malefics, bodes ill.

Obviously these Fortunes must be worked along the ecliptic, in the "Most Accepted Way" or "Degree of Arc Method", outlined in Chapter IV.

Following is a list of Fortunes discovered since Al-Biruni's time and calculated in the regular manner.

MODERN LIST OF FORTUNES

PART OF	FORMULA	FOR NIGHT BIRTHS
FIRST HOUSE		
1 Life or Hyleg (Gadbury)	Asc. + New or Full Moon Prior to Birth − Moon	Don't Change
SECOND HOUSE		
2 Finances	Asc. + Ruler of 2nd Cusp	Don't Change
3 Profession, Mastery, Possessions, Inheritance & Heritage	Asc. + Moon − Saturn	Don't Change
4 Property Management	Asc. + Venus − Sun	Don't Change

No new third house Fortunes uncovered

FOURTH HOUSE		
5 Stability (Faithfullness— M.E. Jones)	Asc. + Saturn − Mercury	Don't Change
6 Disappointment, Endings	Asc. + Mars − Venus	Don't Change
FIFTH HOUSE		
7 Play, Activity, Rapid Change & Variety	Asc. + Venus − Mars	Change for Women
8 Speculation	Asc. + 5th Cusp − Jupiter	Change
9 Art (Venture— M.E. Jones)	Asc. + Mercury − Venus	Change
10 Offspring (M.E. Jones)	Asc. + Moon − Venus	Change
11 Male Children	Asc. + Moon − Jupiter	Change
12 Male Children (Ivy M.G. Jacobson) (Dependence— M.E. Jones)	Asc. + Jupiter − Moon	Change
13 Desire & Sexual Attraction	Asc. + 5th Cusp − Ruler of 5th	Don't Change

(continued)

PART OF	FORMULA	FOR NIGHT BIRTHS
14 Energy, Sex Drive & Stimulation (Borkowski)	Asc. + Pluto − Venus	Don't Change
15 Passion (Destruction— M.E. Jones)	Asc. + Mars − Sun	Don't Change
16 Passion, Emotion & Affection	Asc. + Mars − Venus	Don't Change

No new sixth house Fortunes uncovered

SEVENTH HOUSE

17 Astrology	Asc. + Mercury − Uranus	Don't Change
18 Love & Marriage	Asc. + Venus − Jupiter	Don't Change

EIGHTH HOUSE

19 Life (Female)	Asc. + Moon − Full Moon Prior to Birth	Don't Change
20 Life (Male)	Asc. + Moon − New Moon Prior to Birth	Don't Change
21 Peril & Most Perilous Year	Asc. + Ruler of 8th − Saturn	Don't Change
22 Peril (P. Grell)	Asc. + 8th Cusp − Saturn	Don't Change
23 Occultism (Inspiration M.E. Jones)	Asc. + Neptune − Uranus	Don't Change

NINTH HOUSE

24 Commerce (I.M.G. Jacobson)	Asc. + Mars − Sun	Don't Change
25 Commerce (E. Aldrich) (Vitality—M.E. Jones)	Asc. + Mercury − Sun	Don't Change

continued

PART OF	FORMULA	FOR NIGHT BIRTHS
26 Legalizing (Contracts or Marriage— I.M.G. Jacobson)	9th Cusp + 3rd Cusp − Venus	Don't Change
27 Mind, Understanding, Skill & Intelligence—Male	Asc. + Mars − Mercury	Don't Change
28 Mind, Understanding, Skill & Intelligence— Female	Asc. + Moon − Venus	Don't Change
29 Travel by Land	Asc. + 9th Cusp − Ruler of 9th	Don't Change
30 Travel by Air	Asc. + Uranus − Cusp of House Uranus occupies	Don't Change

TENTH HOUSE

31 Destiny (Z. Dobyns)	M.C. + Sun − Moon	Change
32 Vocation & Status	M.C. + Moon − Sun	Change
33 Honor & Nobility—Day	Asc. + 19° Aries − Sun	Don't Change
34 Honor & Nobility—Night	Asc. + 3° Taurus − Moon	Don't Change
35 Organization (Miracles— E. Aldrich)	Asc. + Pluto − Sun	Don't Change
36 Divorce	Asc. + Venus − 7th Cusp	Don't Change
37 Ostracism & Loss (P. Grell) (Bigotry—M.E. Jones)	Asc. + Uranus − Sun	Don't Change

ELEVENTH HOUSE

38 Friends (Dramatization— M.E. Jones)	Asc. + Moon − Uranus	Change
39 Tragedy (I.M.G. Jacobson)	Asc. + Saturn − Sun	Don't Change

continued

PART OF	FORMULA	FOR NIGHT BIRTHS

TWELFTH HOUSE

PART OF	FORMULA	FOR NIGHT BIRTHS
40 Race & Race Consciousness	Asc. + Moon – Pluto	Change
41 Bondage & Slavery	Asc. + Moon – Moon's Dispositer	Change
42 Imprisonment, Sorrow & Captivity	Asc. + Fortuna – Neptune	Don't Change
43 Perversion (Fascination— M.E. Jones)	Asc. + Venus – Uranus	Don't Change
44 Self-Undoing	Asc. + 12th Cusp – Neptune	Don't Change
45 Treachery, Self Entrapment (Madness—M.E. Jones)	Asc. + Neptune – Sun	Don't Change
46 Bereavement (I.M.G. Jacobson)	12th Cusp + Ruler of 12th – Neptune	Don't Change
47 Suicide	Asc. + 8th Cusp – Neptune	Don't Change
48 Suicide	Asc. + Jupiter – 12th	Don't Change
49 Suicide (Behest— M.E. Jones)	Asc. + Jupiter – Neptune	Don't Change
50 Assassination	Mars + Neptune – Uranus	Don't Change
51 Assassination (I.M.G. Jacobson)	Asc. + Ruler of 12th – Neptune	Don't Change

The Degree of Assassination is 24° Leo-Aquarius. To activate this degree one must have Sun, Moon, Ascendant or one of the parts of Assassination *ON* this degree. Other significators on this degree warn the native to be guarded in public and private affairs, as the degree tends to make the native emotionally offensive.

FORTUNES NOT ASSOCIATED WITH HOUSES

PART OF	FORMULA	FOR NIGHT BIRTHS
52 Cancer—the disease (Emylu Lander Hughes) (Visitation—M.E. Jones)	Asc. + Neptune – Jupiter	Don't Change
53 Catastrophe (I.M.G.Jacobson) (Confidence—M.E. Jones)	Asc. + Uranus – Saturn	Don't Change
54 Foolhardiness (M.E. Jones)	Asc. + Saturn – Uranus	Don't Change
55 Release, Luck (M.E. Jones)	Asc. + Mercury – Mars	Don't Change
56 Benevolence, Assurance (M.E. Jones)	Asc. + Jupiter – Mercury	Don't Change
57 Sensitivity (M.E. Jones)	Asc. + Mercury – Jupiter	Don't Change
58 Aptness, Aloofness (M.E. Jones)	Asc. + Mercury – Saturn	Don't Change
59 Charm, Personality (M.E. Jones)	Asc. + Uranus – Neptune	Don't Change
60 Faith & Good Manners (Gadbury) Cooperation (M.E. Jones)	Asc. + Moon – Mercury	Change
61 Temperament (M.E. Jones)	Asc. + Sun – Mercury	Don't Change
62 Security (M.E. Jones)	Asc. + Venus – Mercury	Don't Change
63 Originality (M.E. Jones)	Asc. + Uranus – Mercury	Don't Change
64 Eccentricity (M.E. Jones)	Asc. + Mercury – Uranus	Don't Change

continued

PART OF	FORMULA	FOR NIGHT BIRTHS
65 Divination (M.E. Jones)	Asc. + Neptune − Mercury	Don't Change
66 Intrusion (M.E. Jones)	Asc. + Mercury − Neptune	Don't Change
67 Negotiation (M.E. Jones)	Asc. + Mars − Jupiter	Don't Change
68 Discord (Gadbury) Controversy (M.E. Jones)	Asc. + Jupiter − Mars	Don't Change
69 Coincidence (M.E. Jones)	Asc. + Mars − Uranus	Don't Change
70 Unpreparedness (M.E. Jones)	Asc. + Uranus − Mars	Don't Change
71 Popularity (M.E. Jones)	Asc. + Mars − Neptune	Don't Change
72 Misunderstanding (M.E. Jones)	Asc. + Neptune − Mars	Don't Change
73 Sentiment (M.E. Jones)	Asc. + Venus − Jupiter	Don't Change
74 Loneliness (M.E. Jones)	Asc. + Jupiter − Venus	Don't Change
75 Success in Investment (M.E. Jones)	Asc. + Venus − Saturn	Don't Change
76 Labor (M.E. Jones)	Asc. + Saturn − Venus	Don't Change
77 Wastefulness (M.E. Jones)	Asc. + Uranus − Venus	Don't Change
78 Vanity (M.E. Jones)	Asc. + Venus − Neptune	Don't Change
79 Corruptness (M.E. Jones)	Asc. + Neptune − Venus	Don't Change
80 Initiative (M.E. Jones)	Asc. + Sun − Mars	Don't Change
81 Memory (M.E. Jones)	Asc. + Mars − Moon	Change
82 Disassociation (M.E. Jones)	Asc. + Moon − Mars	Change
83 Beauty (M.E. Jones)	Asc. + Venus − Sun	Don't Change

continued

PART OF	FORMULA	FOR NIGHT BIRTHS
84 Disinterest, Boredom (M.E. Jones)	Asc. + Sun − Venus	Don't Change
85 Brethren (Gadbury) Allegiance (M.E. Jones)	Asc. + Saturn − Sun	Don't Change
86 Accomplishment (M.E. Jones)	Asc. + Sun − Jupiter	Don't Change
87 Influence (M.E. Jones)	Asc. + Saturn − Moon	Change
88 Impression (M.E. Jones)	Asc. + Jupiter − Sun	Don't Change
89 Caution (M.E. Jones)	Asc. + Neptune − Saturn	Don't Change
90 Timidity (M.E. Jones)	Asc. + Saturn − Neptune	Don't Change
91 Entertainment (M.E. Jones)	Asc. + Uranus − Jupiter	Don't Change
92 Bequest (M.E. Jones)	Asc. + Jupiter − Uranus	Don't Change
93 Genius (M.E. Jones)	Asc. + Sun − Neptune	Don't Change
94 Revelation (M.E. Jones)	Asc. + Moon − Neptune	Change
95 Delusion (M.E. Jones)	Asc. + Neptune − Moon	Change
96 Misinterpretation (M.E. Jones)	Asc. + Uranus − Moon	Change
97 Intellectuality (M.E. Jones)	Asc. + Sun − Uranus	Don't Change
98 Sex (for use in Conception & Prenatal Charts to determine the sex of the child to be born.) Also of some help in charts where sex is unknown.)	M.C. + Asc. − Moon	Needs to be tested
99 Manifestation is Consistency *	Asc. + Moon − Sun + 12^2 + Pi	

* This last one came to me from a student of one of the Rudhyar-based schools and is very esoteric. I don't claim to understand it, but present it for your study. It is supposed to have something to do with the complexity of life rather than its simplicity. In the chart, it is supposed to be either obstacle or release, depending on the individual's development.

SYMBOLS

The symbols for the Fortunes can get very fancy and many astrologers have their own method of signifying them in the chart. Often it is an initial encased in a circle, square, triangle or diamond. Still, some symbols are almost universally understood; these are as follows:

FORTUNA	⊗(Spirit encompassing Matter constructively)
SPIRIT	◯(Spirit supported on Matter)
HEART, LOVE & TRICKERY	♡(The Heart)
COMMERCE	☿(The Caduceus)
PASSION	✕(The Dagger)
INCREASE	♑(The Pomegranate)
TREACHERY	♄(The Trident or Pitchfork)
CATASTROPHY	⚡(The Lightening Flash)
DESTINY	✸(The Buddhic Wheel of Life)
EARTH	⊕(Spirit encompassing active Matter)
DEATH	Ⓓor X (D for Death or X for crossing out & poison)
SUICIDE	⤢(X for Poison plus S for Suicide)
FATE	⧖ (The Hourglass)
INHERITANCE	♈(The Fountain)
IMPRISONMENT	⑦(The Whip)
ILLUMINATION	♌(The Flame)

Any Fortune using the Sun or Moon in its computation should be reversed for a night birth, as the Moon rules all night births and the Sun rules all day births. Still, many of the modern Fortunes ignore this obvious rule. I suggest it should be tested out in practice. Also, when any minus planet is combust (or conjunct) the plus planet, perhaps another planet of similar vibration should be substituted. This too should be tested out in many charts before final acceptance or rejection is set into a rule.

Chapter IV
THE METHODS

There are three main methods to figure the Fortunes, to which I will add a fourth with my Fortune Finder in the back of this book. The first two methods are the most popular but give only occasional accuracy and dependability in reading the chart. Perhaps this is why the Fortunes have fallen into disrepute among astrologers in general. The third method is the Method of the Ancients, which gave them their amazing predictions, impossible today. The Fortune Finder will not give minute accuracy, but it can be an invaluable aid in locating the degree of a Fortune in misreading. Read them all over and test them out, before deciding which method you will use. This way it will be your own impartial decision.

1 THE MOST ACCEPTED WAY

In these first two methods you can check yourself by the simple method of distance along the ecliptic. The Fortune you are working must be as far away from the initial cusp or planet (ascendant, midheaven or other) as the two planets and/or cusps used in the formula are distant from each other, and *in the direction* that the plus planet or cusp is from the minus planet or cusp. If this is not true you have made an error somewhere in your computations. Perhaps you have miscounted the zodiacal degrees between the planets or cusps. Check and re-check until you are sure of yourself.

Use and familiarity will make the method you choose simple and easy to you.

This first method is the "sign, degree and minute" method. Here each sign is assigned a number in its natural rotation around the zodiac. With the sign Aries no degrees of the zodiac have been passed, so Aries is called 0 unless you have to subtract from it. Then you consider Aries as the end of Pisces and call it all 12 signs of the zodiac.

Aries = 0 or 12	Libra = 6
Taurus = 1	Scorpio = 7
Gemini = 2	Sagittarius = 8
Cancer = 3	Capricorn = 9
Leo = 4	Aquarius = 10
Virgo = 5	Pisces = 11

In other words their number is one number less than the house they naturally rule.

This method, while the most accepted way, is the most prone to error because there are so many things to remember. You will see what I mean in a moment.

Let us take a hypothetical chart with the Ascendant at 25° ♉ 27′ the Moon at 28° ♊ 32′ and the Sun at 14° ♓ 09′. The rule for Fortuna (day birth) is Ascendant, plus Moon, minus Sun. Using the sign's number instead of the sign itself, our computation will look like this:

Ascendant	1 Sign 25° 27′
Moon	+ 2 Sign 28° 32′
First sum	3 Sign 53° 59′
Sun	− 11 Sign 14° 09′

We must stop here and add 12 (all the signs) to our first sum (3 Signs 53° 59′) in order to subtract the 11 sign of the Sun.

While we are stopped, we can subtract 30° from the 53° of our first sum because it is obvious that we are going to wind up with more than a 30° answer. Since that equals one full sign, we will add one more sign to the sign column.

continued

	3 Sign 53° 59 '
Whole zodiac	+ 12 Sign
to avoid another extra step later	+ 1 Sign − 30°
Corrected first sum for	
practicality	16 Sign 23° 59 '
Sun	− 11 Sign 14° 09 '
Final sum	5 Sign 09° 50 '

The 5th sign is Virgo, so this Fortuna is at 9° ♍ 50 '

Let us take a second hypothetical problem chart. The Ascendant is 3°♎47 ', the Moon at 6°♏03 ' and the Sun at 23° ♊ 52 '.

Ascendant	6 Sign 3° 47 '
Moon	+ 7 Sign 6° 03 '
First sum	13 Sign 9° 50 '
Sun	− 2 Sign 23° 52 '

We must stop here and borrow 30° (one full sign) from the sign column in order to subtract 23 from 9. Then to subtract 52 from 50, we will have to borrow one degree (60 ') from the degree column and add it to the minute column.

First sum	13 Sign 09° 50 '
Adjustment #1	− 1 Sign + 30°
1st Correction of 1st sum	12 Sign 39° 50 '
Adjustment #2	− 1° + 60 '
Corrected 1st sum	12 Sign 38° 110 '
Sun	− 2 Sign 23° 52 '
Final sum	10 Sign 15° 58 '

The 10th sign is Aquarius, so this Fortuna will be 15° ♒ 58 '.

These are particularly tricky examples and you may do many charts before you run into their equal or trickier. I gave these examples for the purpose of demonstrating how much must be mentally juggled in the "Most Accepted Way". If you are tired or, as most of us are, in a hurry to get your chart done and read, it is very easy to slip up with this method of calculation.

2 DEGREE OF ARC METHOD

I find less fault with this method. It has the advantage of using the arc of the zodiac, which you must know in other phases of astrological mathematics where the sign method has been found to be invalid or confusing. This method does not necessitate the addition of a process to be used only for the fortunes, because you will use it elsewhere.

Here we take the degrees from the 360° wheel. If it is necessary to add anything to the first column, it is always 360°. Here, as in the "Most Accepted Way", Aries is either the beginning or the end.

Aries	= 0° or 360°	Libra	= 180°
Taurus	= 30°	Scorpio	= 210°
Gemini	= 60°	Sagittarius	= 240°
Cancer	= 90°	Capricorn	= 270°
Leo	= 120°	Aquarius	= 300°
Virgo	= 150°	Pisces	= 330°

With this method you become familiar with how far around the zodiac each sign is by degree. This will take the fear out of some of the advanced astrological computations you will run into later in your studies.

All that is done here is to eliminate the factor of the signs. We are dealing now strictly with degrees and minutes. For convenience, until they are automatic, list the above degrees of the signs on a hand-sized card or wheel and carry it with your materials for chart computation.

Now, let's take those tricky ones I gave you under the previous method:

(Ascendant (♉ = 30° + 25° 27 ')	55° 27 ' of zodiac
Moon (♊ = 60° 28°32 ')	+ 88° 32 ' of zodiac
First sum	143° 59 ' of zodiac
To subtract, add whole zodiac	+ 360°
Adjusted first sum	503° 59 '
Sun (♓ = 330° + 14°09 ')	− 344° 09 ' of zodiac
Final sum	159° 50 ' of zodiac
Virgo is nearest and lesser at	− 150°
So Fortuna will be in Virgo	9° 50 ' ♍

We get the same answer (we had better!) but we have eliminated the juggling of the signs. In doing this we have overcome one more possibility of error.

continued

That second problem works out like this;

Ascendant (♎ = 180° + 3°47′)	183° 47′ of zodiac
Moon (♏ = 210° + 6°03′) =	216° 03′ of zodiac
First sum	399° 50′
Borrow 1° and add 60′	−1° +60′
Adjusted first sum	398° 110′
Sun (♊ = 60° + 23°52′)	−83° 52′ of zodiac
Final sum	315° 58′ of zodiac
Aquarius is nearest and less at	−300°
So Fortuna is in Aquarius	15° 58′ ♒

Again we get the same answer but with less juggling.

3 THE METHOD OF THE ANCIENTS

Because this method may be new to many of you, I will give its background first, then I will give you the tight method of computation. Please bear with me and keep in mind that I'm not asking you to do all of these things. They are merely things you must understand or you won't know why you are using this method.

This is the only method that takes into consideration that the Fortunes are not planets out in space beaming down on us. In actuality they are earthly computations to find an earthly reaction point of the planets, not obvious in the zodiacal aspects.

These computations will not come out the same as figuring the other two ways, unless you are doing a chart very near the Earth's Equator. The two previous methods use *zodiacal distance* (along the ecliptic) as their measuring stick. This method uses *mundane* (or earthly) *distance*. Since we are born, live and to all intents and purposes operate mostly on the mundane-physical level, I am led to believe that this is the true method. But test it out for yourself. Work with it, read it in your charts, compare it with the other methods and see which one is most satisfactory and dependable, in relation to the actual life of the person, place or thing for which you are reading the chart.

Many astrologers bemoan that so much important information has been lost through the ages because of inaccurate recording, catastrophe and forgeries. They know that old Chaldean and Egyptian astrologers were able to make predictions far in advance of events, a task impossible today.

Not all, but many of the answers these astrologers seek, are to be found in the Fortunes *if they are worked correctly*. The Ancients did record their knowledge accurately. They recorded it in such a way that it would be overlooked by the uninitiate. The Fortune's formulas were recorded something like this; "So and so, plus this, minus that, equals. . .Eureka!"

All the initiated knew what that meant. To the uninitiated, it meant what it said. In about four out of ten cases, it seemed to work, but not enough to be the dependable tool the Ancients knew it was. Of all the methods of working the Fortunes, only this Method of the Ancients could possibly be the way the Ancients gained such impressive results in guiding the lives, nations and history of ages past.

Mr. Wynn (Sidney K. Bennett) calls them *Equilibrium parts*. This is the clue and explanation of this method. A chart with the Fortunes computed in this way becomes a multi-dimensional chart, not just a three-dimensional chart. The computation ignores such things as intercepted signs and one sign ruling two houses. It follows the ancient practice of *equilibrium charts*, which of course is mundane, not zodiacal distance.

My research discovered that SUBTRACT turns out to be the code word meaning: MOVE TO THE NEGATIVE, RECEPTIVE OR MINUS POSITION OF THE ASCENDANT. The word ADD turns out to be the code word for: FIND THE HOUSE THAT IS BEING POSITIVELY AND AGGRESSIVELY ACTIVATED IN THAT EQUILIBRIUM CHART, and what action, if any, it is giving to or receiving from the Ascendant in the natal chart.

An equilibrium chart is a chart with the sign, degree and minute of one of the planets placed on the Ascendant. All the remaining cusps have the same degree and minute with all the signs in their proper order, making each house an *EQUAL* thirty degrees and no minutes.

continued

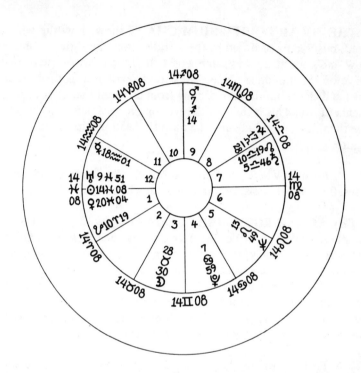

A solar equilibrium chart of our first hypothetical problem (which could have happened on March 5, 1922) would look something like this. Fortuna *must be located in the third house, roughly fourteen degrees in from the third house cusp*, no matter what time of the daylight hours the native was born or where in the world he was born, because the Moon in this solar equilibrium chart is fourteen degrees and twenty-two minutes inside of this solar equilibrium chart's third house.

Before I give the "tight computation formula," let's investigate the possible equilibrium charts. Everyone who has used a solar equilibrium chart knows how valuable it is in character analysis and in finding the key to the person's will. But what about Moon equilibriums, Mercury equilibriums, Venus equilibriums, etc.? We can even do cuspal equilibriums, using the angles or the house which shows the problem or points of concentration, not to mention equilibrium charts of the more powerful Fortunes themselves (those involving the Sun and Moon especially). What could charts like this tell us about the native, place or event?

1 THE SOLAR EQUILIBRIUM CHART shows how the will is used, misused or confused by the world around the native. It shows how one's ego faces that same world. It is the chart of the primal drive on the mundane plane. The aspects exist just as they did in the natal chart, but they are coming from different houses or departments of life. This is the way the will or ego sees them and tries to use them. This also indicates the native's relationship with a father figure.

A Fortune where the Sun is subtracted indicates ouside considerations which assist or challenge the will or ego.

2 THE LUNAR EQUILIBRIUM CHART shows how the rest of the planets assist or afflict the native's emotional life and stability and why, emotionally, they assign them other values than what are obviously right; the emotional nature sees their influences coming from different departments (houses). This is how the personality will attract or repel the people the natives meet in particular and in the general public. This chart tells much about their relationship with the mother figure and other women in general.

A Fortune where the Moon is subtracted indicates outside pressures which try to mold the emotions for good or ill, trying to find a response or reaction in the emotional nature, depending on the native's particular phase of emotional control, spiritual development and understanding.

3 THE MERCURY EQUILIBRIUM CHART shows how the mental capabilities will want to face life's problems and triumphs. This chart can indicate mental problems or superior advantages. The indications of mental balance and imbalance are nicely delineated here and their source becomes obvious.

A Fortune where Mercury is subtracted shows the special influences that are molding the mind and thought processes of the individual toward reality, fantasy or aberration.

4 THE VENUS EQUILIBRIUM CHART shows the love life of the man, the type of woman he is looking for and what he expects from her in **all** ways. If badly afflicted it could indicate a preference for men. For the woman, this is the chart of what she thinks of herself as a female and also her degree of acceptance or rejection of other women. For both men and women, this is the chart that shows their sense of values, their basic morals and where they are or are not materialistic or earthbound.

The Fortune where Venus is subtracted shows the path of least resistance that the child will most likely follow in forming its values or lack of values. If this chart causes alarm, the parents, teachers or guardians may make the easy way difficult and help the child to shape up in a more socially acceptable fashion. It would be an interesting experiment, at least.

5 THE MARS EQUILIBRIUM CHART shows what the man thinks of himself as a male, what his sexual organs are like and what he enjoys doing with them. This is the material evidence he feels he either has or lacks in backing up his own self-image. In the woman's chart, this shows the type of man she wants and what she expects from him in **all** ways. For both man and woman, this chart shows their ability to organize or dissipate their mental, physical, emotional and even sometimes the spiritual energies, and how these energies will be dispersed. This is especially true if Mars is in bad aspect, because it could force the native to seek beneath the surface appearance of things and discover the sources. This is the chart of how the energies will be used to attain the will's goals.

A Fortune where Mars is subtracted shows the outer forces that are impinging on the native's development and expression of the energies. The aspects in the natal chart will indicate the levels of expression easily open to them.

6 THE JUPITER EQUILIBRIUM CHART shows how the good things in life will come into the life or event promised by the chart. It indicates the native's ability to accept growth, expansion, stability, comfort and the responsibility these things involve. It can also show the blocks and excuses the native will use to avoid these things; the feelings of unworthiness and how the responsibilities seem to outweigh the benefits.

A Fortune where Jupiter is subtracted indicates how the natives will react to expansive ideas and ideals and what will make them react perversely to expansion.

7 THE SATURN EQUILIBRIUM CHART indicates the maturity and weakness in the make-up of the natives, their inability to face maturity or the overconfidence which makes them bite off more than they can chew. This chart shows how they will face life's problems or hide from them. It tells what they have already learned and honed into practical working tools, which others may think of as superiority, or what the person is frantically trying to avoid facing.

A Fortune where Saturn is subtracted shows the influences that are at work to force the natives into a more mature outlook and the restrictions they will have to face realistically as they learn the differences between humility and the helplessness of martyrdom and self-pity.

8 THE URANUS EQUILIBRIUM CHART indicates the individual uniqueness, the quirks of genius or madness which separates the native from all other similar beings. It tells of the native's inventiveness, whether as a spiritual leader, a space flight visionary or simply gossiping with a flair. This chart gives the clue as to how the native can release any overpowering destructive or overly negative vibrations. Release often occurs through shock and changes the native will not willingly accept; but it brings the release and pulls out the blocks which have been "protecting" the native from a better way of life.

The Fortune where Uranus is subtracted shows the special and individual quirks of nature which impress upon the natives the need for and the ways to use their abstract mind in relationship to logic, which is often illogical—but it works.

9 THE NEPTUNE EQUILIBRIUM CHART shows what the person is trying to avoid seeing in a realistic light. It is the higher sense of idealism, fatalism, universal love and/or fear. This chart can pinpoint the blind spots the person has accepted. The aspects indicate how these blind spots can be used and applied and what kind of sugar is needed for bait to get the native to accept a more realistic, dogmatic or universal view of things. Conversely, this chart shows the individual's capacity or incapacity to accept spiritual realities. These are the outer influences which buffet or assist the person's basic spiritual reality and unshakable convictions, no matter how badly expressed, which help to mold their illogical destiny.

The Fortune where Neptune is subtracted shows the solid ground controlled by the native or the swamp into which they are sinking.

10 THE PLUTO EQUILIBRIUM CHART shows the ability of the natives to organize their lives into a homogeneous unit or a hopeless mess. This shows what is dispensable and indispensable; what they feel they can kill off and what they absolutely need to build on. Here is their view of their indiscretions and the roots of their personal discrimination. Laid open here is the vision they have of the Cosmic Pattern or Mind, their ability to comprehend it and the influences which are moving inexorably to conclusion, often a conclusion the native is not aware of. This is the chart of the native's higher goal or plan and the path and obstacles involved in its completion.

The Fortune where Pluto is subtracted indicates events which have an almost fated quality about them, unless the person is willing to make the supreme effort to understand and exercise his own control or conscious cooperation. Unfortunately, these events invariably are of the exact nature the person feels least capable of fighting or handling. Usually there are many cries of "Woe is me!" and they philosophically let the event plow them under.

11 THE MIDHEAVEN EQUILIBRIUM CHART indicates the native's ability or inability to cope with the world face-to-face and accept the responsibility for their own actions, both blame and rewards. This indicates the ability to face up to their own goals and find a way to make them socially acceptable, if they are not. Here is the ultimate test the natives will be put through on the material-social level and it often verges into and merges with their inner spiritual awareness. This often opens up new and further goals of personal achievement, or their failure to recognize the new goals.

The Fortune with the Midheaven subtracted would be an indication of the help or hindrance available in realizing the native's goals.

23 THE NORTH NODE EQUILIBRIUM CHART shows the pathway to adventure and growth on an emotional-soul level. Here are the potentials to be stabilized into dependable working tools; how to develop advantages and abundance. This is putting the native's next step of spiritual growth into a down to earth map.

At this time there are no Fortunes which use the north node. Speculation suggests that if the north node were subtracted, it would indicate a means or way of unlocking the consciousness on an emotional level to gain a long-view perspective of the native as an evolving entity, rather than just a social personality.

13 THE SOUTH NODE EQUILIBRIUM CHART shows the pathway which the evolving entity has already trod. These are the tools already developed, which do not need redeveloping; the old familiar habits and vices the natives kid themselves into thinking are their due. This is the map of past advantages taken without work or merit, where a balance has been upset. This chart shows the various ways in which the balance may be reestablished, if the imbalance is not to become an impediment to the person's progress.

At this time there are no Fortunes which use the south node. Speculation suggests that if the south node were subtracted, it would indicate habits, emotions and thoughts that must be put in second place to make allowance for new emotional and mental development and the long-range perspective by which people may weed out their pathway in life. The south node and the north node equilibrium charts, together would show how balance and harmony can be brought into existence within the individual, regardless of the disharmony and imbalance of the world around the native.

14 THE LILITH EQUILIBRIUM CHART indicates the area of life wherein lies personal horror, that which holds the person in superstitious awe, fear or shame. Here is the **thing(s)** the person will literally do anything to avoid facing openly. Here is where personal ignorance, pride and prejudice are most strongly entrenched, which the individual externalizes onto others. Conversely, if the native is strong enough or badly cornered enough to be brought face to face with these elements, it can be a soul releasing experience. The boogieman in the closet is discovered to be only a Raggedy Ann doll or a tin soldier the natives forgot they left there. The fears and inhibitions of a lifetime (or more) are sloughed off, allowing the person to be truly young, effervescent and alive. These things are almost never of a material or social nature, but things of a spiritual nature. If they are faced and dealt with, it is not uncommon to discover that the native possesses some non-apparent gift like clairvoyance, clairaudience, etc.

At this time there are no Fortunes that use Lilith. Many astrologers will not even consider that she exists, although astronomers list her as Asteroid *#1181.* If a Fortune subtracted Lilith, it is suggested that it would have to do with death by fright, the trigger being the one image the individual feared or was repulsed by the most or the uncovering of the native's latent spiritual powers.

15 THE LULU EQUILIBRIUM CHART shows how to handle horror beyond the native's tolerance. For the purpose of accomplishment, here is the ability to blank out reality which, when under stress, the native is incapable of handling. This is an unrealistic approach to life for realistic ends, turning on the native's euphoria in the face of overwhelming odds to bring about the blessedness of fulfillment beyond the possible endurance of the native.

Fewer astrologers are willing to admit the existence of Lulu than will admit Lilith. I do not know the catalogue number of this "fairy godmother" influence. No Fortunes use Lulu at this time, but speculation suggests that if Lulu were subtracted, it would be an indicator of ease of accomplishment in improbable areas.

16 THE FORTUNA EQUILIBRIUM CHART shows where and how the person or event is consciously most comfortable, how the will, emotions and personality blend to take advantage of the good and handle the bad operating in the life. As in all Equilibrium charts, it is the focus on how best to unlock the planet, cusp or part's fullest potential in the most constructive way and handle the obstacles in the path of that fulfillment.

A Fortune where Fortuna is subtracted has to do with the fulfillment of an objective relating to the will, emotions and personality.

17 THE PART OF SPIRIT EQUILIBRIUM CHART indicates the basic raw material of Universal or Spiritual Energy available to the native, when all material illusion is stripped away. This tells how other things conspire to make the natives aware (or unaware) of their soul-level basic drives. Here is the ability or inability to gain access to the highest single unit or monad of the native's being.

A Fortune where Spirit is subtracted in an indication of the pathway to follow and the obstacles in the way of the natives discovering their inner motivation and true spiritual identity.

No one expects you to do all of those Equilibrium Charts. The concept of equilibrium charts is part of the Method of the Ancients. All you have to do is be aware of their existence and remember one or two keywords for the planets most often subtracted in the Fortunes you find useful. No one ever works all the points, just the ones that may have a bearing on the life or the question posed by the chart to be read.

A chart with the Fortunes computed the ancient way is a chart with all those equilibrium charts laid over it. That could be a pretty confusing mass to read, unless your chart is as big as Dodger Stadium. Each Fortune marks a planetary placement from one of those equilibrium charts. You can see at a glance how those planetary *shades* or *shadows* are being affected by your natal, progressed, directed or transiting planets. In other words they help to give you access to the inner plane motivations and causes underneath the composite manifested effect, which we call reality.

If one of these nonmaterial receptors falls in the path of a fixed star, it becomes much more powerful. Often it can appear to be an active element in the chart instead of just a sensitive point. The fixed star (the constant spiritual motivation which our planets play against) tends to take over the Fortune, giving it the activity and disposition of the star. This, then, is another factor that makes the nonobservant astrologer say the Fortunes do not work.

The use of single equilibrium charts gives us a cockeyed view of the native, place or event, which can lead to a downward path of destruction or black magic perspectives. By using the important points in the various equilibrium charts as fortunes in the natal chart, forces us to be constantly aware of the whole person, place or event, and the constant interreactions of the various levels. This way you are in a multi-dimensional world, seeing and reading from every level of action, reaction and quintessence of all factors involved.

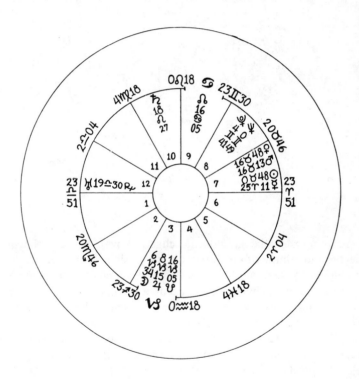

In *Wynn's Magazine* of January 1946, Mr. Wynn expounds on the equilibrium method using Adolph Hitler's chart and what he refers to as the Sun-Jupiter Part. You will recognize this as the Part of Increase and Recognition. As Mr. Wynn gave only degrees on the intermediate house cusps, I have reworked the above birth chart for Adolph Hitler.

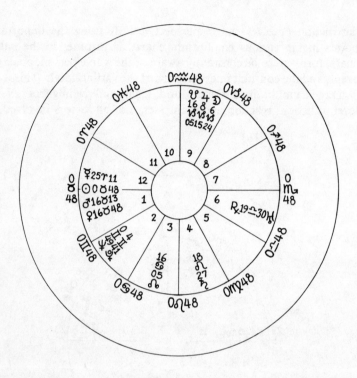

Doing the solar equilibrium chart (above), we have the sign, degree and minute of the Sun (0° ♉ 48 ') rising. Jupiter in this chart is at 8° ♑ 15 ' and falls in the ninth house, which only held the north node in the birth chart. As you become familiar with this concept, you will automatically be able to see what sign falls on which cusp, thereby locating your plus planet.

Wynn's method for finding the exact position of the desired part is to find what *proportion* of the *natal house* corresponds to the planet's position (here, Jupiter) in the *equilibrium house*. We find the equilibrium proportion (E.P.) by subtracting the ninth house equilibrium cusp of 0° ♑ 48 ' from Jupiter's degree and minute. If the planet were closer to the tenth house cusp, we would use that cusp instead.

	Jupiter	8° ♑ 15 '
	Eq. 9th Cusp	−0° ♑ 48 '
E.P.		7° 27 '

In Hitler's natal chart there is 23° Ⅱ 30′ on the ninth house cusp, all the sign of Cancer intercepted and 0° ♌ 18′ on the midheaven, giving a total of 36° 48′ (almost 37°) in the natal ninth house. As 7°27′ is to 30° (of equilibrium house), so will the natal proportion (N.P) be to 37° (or 36°48′)

Use the regular logarithm tables found in the back of most ephemerides to work this out. Because the tables do not go beyond 16° to 24°, you will have to change the house degrees into minutes. Since you will do this both going into the logarithm and coming out, rest assured that you will be getting the correct answer.

E.P.	7° 27′ = Log of	.5081	
Nat. House (almost 37°)	37′ = Log of	+ 1.5902	
First Log of		2.0983	
Equilib. House (30°)	30′ = Log of	− 1.6821	
Final Log of		.4162 = 9°12′ N.P.	

Add this 9° 12′ to Hitler's natal ninth house cusp of 23 Ⅱ 30′ and the Sun-Jupiter Part will be at 2° ♋ 42′, over 13° away from the natal north node. This is really too far away for timing of any event or confusing the node for the Sun-Jupiter part.

If you like a little more exactitude, use J. Allen Jones, Jr.'s five point easy tables, which allow you to change the minutes into seconds (as you changed the degrees into minutes). With these tables, our above computation would look like this;

E.P.	7° 27′ = Log of	.50806	
Nat. House (36° 48′)	36′ 48″ = Log of	+ 1.59251	
First Log of		2.10057	
Equilib. House (30°)	30′ = Log of	− 1.68124	
Final Log of		.41933	
		= 9° 08′ N.P.	
Natal Ninth Cusp		+ 23 Ⅱ 30	
Sun-Jupiter Part at		2 ♋ 38	

Mr. Wynn gives us most compelling proof with his delineation of this placement in Hitler's chart. It is good because there is nothing in the natal ninth close enough to be confused with this degree.

Some say Hitler was politically dead after the middle of 1944 . Certainly he made no public appearances after then. Saturn reached

this Sun-Jupiter Part of August 15, 1944 for the first time in his
political career, after traversing his Fortuna two and a half degrees
earlier. On October 23, 1944, Saturn retrograded, backing over the
Sun-Jupiter Part on January 2, 1945. Finally, Saturn turned direct
just short of Fortuna on March 6, 1945 and went over the Sun-
Jupiter Part for the last time May 4, 1945...*the day Hitler is said to
have disappeared completely!*

Wynn goes into much more detail in the article, which I suggest
you dig out and read at your nearest astrological library.

Remember, if the planet in the equilibrium chart is more than
halfway (15°) closer to the next house cusp, use *that* succeeding
cusp, rather than the cusp of the house the planet falls in. Then *subtract* your answer (N.P.) from the succeeding house cusp instead of
adding it as we did in the Hitler chart. Even Mr. Jones' tables only
goes up to 24°.

When using the fourth method, I suggest that you make some
special lists of the Fortunes for quick reference. That suggestion is
equally valid for the Method of the Ancients. If you are not interested in the minutes of the Fortunes, you can use this Easy
Method with the Fortune Finder located in the back of this book.

4 THE EASY METHOD

If you decide to use the Method of the Ancients, laminate and
use the Fortune Finder in the back of this book. Mark all the natal
planets and cusps on the INSIDE WHEEL with a felt-tipped pen or
grease pencil which can be wiped off with a cloth. On the OUTSIDE
WHEEL, mark your equilibrium Ascendant and all the equilibrium
house cusps. Turn the Fortune Finder around so the equilibrium
Ascendant is on your left (or wherever your method of astrology is
used to dealing with the Ascendant). On the inside wheel, locate the
planet the formula says to add. See what house it falls in on the outside wheel. Mentally do a rough equation of how far that will be,
depending on the size of the natal house it corresponds to, then add
or subtract those degrees to or from the cusp used in the natal
house. At the most you should only be two degrees off. If you can
read a chart well, this variation should make very little difference,
unless you are trying to time an event or influence down to the
minute.

If you choose one of the first two methods, use a plastic coated
aspect finder. Place your natal planets and cusps on the INSIDE

WHEEL with a felt-tipped pen or a grease pencil which can be
wiped off with a cloth. Turn the planet or cusp to be subtracted to
the degree of the natal Ascendant on the OUTSIDE WHEEL. On
the inside wheel, locate the degree of the planet or cusp the formula
says to add. The sign and degree that it lines up with on the outside
wheel is the placement of that Fortuna in the natal, progressed,
horary or whatever chart you are doing.

While this method only gives degrees, it may not be to
everyone's liking. **But do not overlook this method.** Too often in
the middle of an interpretation, things have been brought up that
made me wish I had calculated an extra Fortune or two. While this
Easy Method lacks exactitude, it can be valuable for split-second
positioning of a Fortune in mid-reading. This can bring the aid of
that little extra insight into an overlooked facet of the chart before
you.

Be alert, as *all points are not calculated from the Ascendant.*
There are quite a few Fortunes that use the mid heaven, other cusps
or planets as their starting point. As more spiritual research and
orientation goes on, there will be more of these non-Ascendant Fortunes uncovered. In these cases, place the planet or point to be subtracted on these other starting points instead of the Ascendant.

It is a good idea to make your own lists for this method and the
Method of the Ancients. With each setting of the wheel you will be
able to see at a glance all of the Fortunes you can place without
changing settings. I won't go through all of the Fortunes, but for
the benefit of understanding, I will list the Fortunes which may be
determined by placing the Sun and the Moon on the Ascendant, or
doing a solar or lunar equilibrium chart.

I will leave it up to your own interest to finish up by going
through the composite lists, taking all the points that Mercury is
subtracted from, then Venus, Mars, Jupiter, Saturn, Uranus, Neptune, Pluto, Fortuna, Spirit and finish up with those oddities which
have other points, cusps, degrees, Lords, New and Full Moons or
other things to be subtracted.

*On the inner wheel, mark all the natal planets and house cusps,
with the number of the house. On the outer wheel, mark the degree
of the Sun as the Ascendant. Follow around the wheel marking that
same degree in each sign.*

continued

YOUR PART OF	IN THE NATAL CHART	IS WHERE
Fortuna (day birth)		the Moon is
Spirit (night birth)		the Moon is
Time of Fortune in Marriage		the Moon is
Commerce (Aldrich) (Vitality—M.E. Jones)		Mercury is
Commerce (Jacobson)		Mars is
Heart, Love, Trickery of Men, Intercourse, Deception by Women (day birth)		Venus is
Beauty (M.E. Jones)		Venus is
Passion (Destruction—M.E. Jones)		Mars is
Tradition, Knowledge of Affairs, Fame, Increase & Recognition (day birth)		Jupiter is
Impression (M.E. Jones)		Jupiter is
Operations and Orders in Medical Treatment (day birth)		Jupiter is
Ruler's Victory or Conquest, Love of Brethren, Father, Fatality & Karma (day birth)		Saturn is
(If Saturn be combust)		Jupiter is
Property Management		Venus is
Tragedy (Jacobson)		Saturn is
Catastrophe (Jacobson)		Uranus is
Ostracism & Loss (Grell) (Bigotry—M.E. Jones)		Uranus is
Treachery		Neptune is
Organization (Miracles—Aldrich)		Pluto is
Honorable Acquaintances (night birth)		Fortuna is
Honor & Nobility (day birth)		19° Aries is
Death of Brothers & Sisters		10° of the 3rd House is

continued

On the inner wheel, mark all the natal planets and house cusps, with the number of the house. On the outer wheel, mark the degree of the Moon as the Ascendant. Follow around the wheel marking that same degree in each sign.

YOUR PART OF	IN THE NATAL CHART	IS WHERE
Fortuna (night birth)		the Sun is
Spirit (day birth)		the Sun is
Time of Fortune in Marriage (night birth)		the Sun is
Abundance in the House		the Sun is
Knowledge & Education (night birth)		Mercury is
Timidity, Hiding & Travel (day birth)		Mercury is
Mother & Condition of Female Children (night birth)		Venus is
Daughters & Chastity of Women		Venus is
Marriage of Women (Valens), Misconduct of Women, Deceit of Men by Women & Unchastity of Women		Mars is
Memory (M.E. Jones)		Mars is
Life or Hyleg	New or Full Moon Prior to Birth is	
Male Children (Jacobson) (Dependence—M.E. Jones)		Jupiter is
Influence (M.E. Jones)		Saturn is
Inheritance, Heritage, Profession, Mastery & Possessions (night birth)		Saturn is
Delusion (M.E. Jones)		Neptune is
Misinterpretation (M.E. Jones)		Uranus is
Death		the 8th Cusp is
Honor & Nobility (night birth)		3° of Taurus is
Expected Birth (day birth)	the Lord of the Moon's House is	

Ready check-lists like these make it easy to find the degree of any Fortune at a glance.

Chapter V
FORTUNES IN
THE HOUSES

To go through all the Fortunes would take a complete reference library, so I will only take you through a few of the Fortunes in the houses to give you a feeling of how to read them. With a little practice, you will develop your own "feeling" in your own style of interpretation, which will be entirely different from mine or anything I could teach you. The most important thing to remember is that the Fortunes are not planets; they are *planetary shadows* or *three dimensional aspects*. Because of this, *they cannot aspect another Fortune* except by conjunction. They only receive aspects from planets, nodes, progressions and transits...but that is enough!

First, of course, we will start with Fortuna in the houses, this being the best known Fortune.

FORTUNA — FIRST HOUSE

BASIC

This position brings the native an understanding of people as a mass (remember, it's the Moon's point in a solar chart or the Sun's point in a lunar chart). These natives have the ability to feel what is wanted and needed, making it possible for them to give easily to others. The basic type is happiest when fulfilling the needs of others. There are many worldly contacts and gains through experiences of early life. Can make for a very popular person if the rest of the chart is not too afflicted. This placement brings a fine competitive spirit, good personality and character. These are often the self-made people; their own creation or undoing whichever they make it. All headway is made by their own effort. Often brings success through the use of the physical body, like Jack Dempsey. Under extreme pressure, the emotional release is through contacts with others.

CONSTRUCTIVE
The natives will use their personal abilities for uniting the weak and the strong in their environment; the needy with those who have abundance; reconciling the interests of management and labor. The extreme personal sensitivity (Sun, Moon and Ascendant point in the first house) of these natives, can lead them to give too much of themselves. Must take care of the health and steer clear of extremes of selfishness and unselfishness.

DESTRUCTIVE
Forces life to teach them all its lessons the hard way. If not through bad or unwise choice of companions, then through shady or illegal enterprises. Can be smug, self-satisfied and more than a little egocentric. If they have any looks at all, the mirror may be their best friend.

MATERIAL
The search for happiness in the material world is carried out as though it were a karmic necessity. Demands contact with others, compiling and gathering people around them as though they were the only organizers in the world. This brings great help in early life experiences through friends, parents and teachers; but the ready cash comes through personal effort. If badly afflicted, this can bring disillusionment from these same people, who may appear all to be working against the natives. This can often bring the loss of all the funds they have worked for.

SPIRITUAL
Must overcome an extreme sensitivity to external pressures and influences. Personal experiences are not as important as what the natives are able to learn from them. They should discover early in

life to rely only on themselves and find their own individual mode of expression through personal investigation of the self. If badly afflicted, the native may be called upon to make material sacrifices for each spiritual gain.

HORARY

If Fortuna is unafflicted in the first house, the question will conclude to the querent's best personal interests. Brings both mental and material riches, according to the condition of the querent's significator by both sign and aspect. The better and stronger the ruler, the richer the benefits. If afflicted, the querent must be ready to put forth great personal effort in order to win the point in the matter.

FORTUNA — SECOND HOUSE

BASIC

Much concern for financial matters, security and status through the possessions. Good for personal skills and abilities. Gain through furnishings (upholstery skills, etc.), collections, antiques and souvenir items. Receives help through business friends and associates. Possibility of having a hero worship complex. Brings dealings with money and people in finance and/or economic interests. Basic emotional release is through sex. Thinks of life on the materialistic lines, unless the rest of the chart raises the sights.

CONSTRUCTIVE

Brings a drive for education and self-betterment on all levels. Occult studies could be indicated; anything which has to do with making things manifest from the negative or non-manifest planes. Actively helping for mutual benefit where talent development or money is involved. Usually develops the personal skills for the benefit of the public.

DESTRUCTIVE

Brings a drive for earning power to the exclusion of all else. Associated with dishonest schemes, designed to defraud financially or economically, and if Neptune is involved it could includ "fun-

ny money." Unfortunately, they may get away with it for so long
that they have no other resources to fall back on (the second house
is the house of the Moon's exaltation). They can become despon-
dent, brooding, hyperemotional and suffer from chronic hypochon-
dria.

MATERIAL

Is very fortunate for money, even if under affliction. They have
the drive, endurance and patience to strive for gain through the use
of their own efforts, talents and abilities. This would be a good person to hire as a worker or promoter for a trustworthy enterprise.

SPIRITUAL

Will bring in money and things of value (manifestation) due to
their innate understanding of the Universal Laws of supply. Their
greatest lesson is to learn how to use material things and money for
the benefit of others; not just for themselves alone. Their spiritual
job is to bring spiritual and thought forms into manifestation.

HORARY

If unafflicted, the querents will get money, even though not expecting any. If they are expecting money, they will get more than
they expect. If the question is not about money, they have the
talents and abilities to bring the question to a successful conclusion
by their own efforts. If badly afflicted, the querents should drop the
action, unless it is a matter of principle and they don't care if they
have to work like dogs and then wind up figuring their losses.

FORTUNA — THIRD HOUSE

BASIC

This is the itchy-foot position: interested in travel in all of its
phases, short trips, long trips and even trips to the Moon. This
placement indicates a healthy intererst in literature and dissemination of knowledge. In fact, these are the very people no occult society should allow in their doors. When it comes to wisdom and
knowledge, these people can not help but spread it around to any
and all who need or ask. They don't have time for game-playing, in-

trigue or instigation because they want the "real facts." Then they rush out to dispel falsehoods...as they see it! There is the possibility of public relations for or with a relative. They can idolize (constructively or destructively) a brother or sister figure and make that idealization the foundation of their life pattern.

CONSTRUCTIVE

Teaching the masses through the pen, voice, art or other communication forms. This is the second house to the second house (the expression or results of the talents and abilities). They operate well in the study of science, advertising, travel and being the friend-in-need to neighbors because they know how to leave them alone when they are not needed. Emotional release can come through long journeys and abstract reasoning. If unafflicted, they will receive help from the family and neighbors, which could launch the native in the business of distributing knowledge early in life. Brings great versatility in handling many things at the same time.

DESTRUCTIVE

Dishonesty, misrepresentation of self and/or products. If afflicted, the family and neighbors will demand help but give none in return. In extreme cases they may even ride and badger the natives as being "unable to take charge of their own affiars" (depending on the afflicting planets). There is a danger of being too versatile and spreading themselves too thin. There can be an obsession with communication as a one-way channel, which can easily become thwarted or twisted into maligning gossip.

MATERIAL

Monies can come through the use of the mind, mental pursuits, writing, taking trips or arranging trips for others (travel bureaus etc.) They may be able to borrow money from neighbors, receive cash as a present or legacy. Satisfaction comes through the exercise of the mind and the expression of ideas. Relaxation is more satisfying with relatives or close, family-like friends. Happiest in occupations connected with communication or travel.

SPIRITUAL

They must avoid intellectual vanity (especially if afflicted). The natives should find an outlet by which they can share the riches of their mind with others. This cannot be done selfishly or egotistically as a means of binding others to themselves. They must eventually realize that the richness of experience can transcend the wealth of the mind, as the latter has a tendency to become escapist. They must test out all precepts and ideas in the laboratory of day to day living.

HORARY

If aspected and unafflicted, the querents will benefit by staying in the present locality or climate and communicating their needs to a brother or sister figure. If afflicted, the querents should change neighborhoods, as where they're living is detrimental to the outcome of the question...and they should do it alone!

FORTUNA — FOURTH HOUSE

BASIC

Strong attachments to the security of the domestic circle, be it a humble shack or the international intrigue of a palace. They contact the public through, with or because of a parent (generally the father, but afflictions could produce a strong and pushy "stage mother"). There is an interest in the living conditions of others. The more intellectual types could work in or head a health and welfare department of some type. This position always brings problems. Even though this is the Moon's natural house, the Sun and Moon would have to be in a near-square aspect in order to place Fortuna here. This placement helps to bring out patriotism or dedication to the ideals of childhood, material success, recognition from the profession and reputation (good or bad). These natives find emotional release through status, getting credit for their own or the family's position or through theatrical endeavors.

CONSTRUCTIVE

Could find contentment through the improvement of public properties, real estate, housing development, farming lands, mining or attempting to achieve some type of public security, especially for the aged. This is a very strong position for the accumulation of a personal estate. Pride in heritage, tradition and respect of/and from the family.

DESTRUCTIVE

Shows up as reckless opposition to those in positions of power. A rabble-rousing inclination, dissipation of estates without replacement or reward. Very strong position for a complete disharmony of nature. Self-seeking, self-indulgent, with a tendency toward race superiority and a possible Oedipus complex. Somehow, these people do not want to progress beyond the precepts and ideals of their childhood, so they can fight progress and personal growth. Often their patriotism is of a fanatic leaning.

MATERIAL

Can indicate a wealthy parent. Money through real estate in the native land. May have an imposing and affluent home. Good for finding hidden treasure on the land or among personal family effects. They can be fond of ostentation and showy automobiles. If afflicted, can indicate automobile accidents (the result of second house from the third). Should be wealthy or affluent at the end of life. There is a patriotic regard for the welfare of the native land.

SPIRITUAL

Brings a concern with down-to-earth foundations for spiritual values. Brings good karma through the parents and early training for handling other types of karma. Can't help giving a home to unfortunate relatives, friends and stray animals. They must not allow themselves to get caught up in hoarding wealth or savings for their old age, as there will be more than enough for that. They should concern themselves with philanthropies, endowing homes for the aged or other institutions. Strong parental ties, so they must always be ready to give aid in this sector of life.

HORARY

If unafflicted, the querent will find the lost article in the home, be reunited with loved ones either physically or with momentos and/or inheritances. If strong indications of psychic or spiritual atmosphere exists in the rest of the chart, this position can indicate direct communication with a "departed one". If afflicted; querents lost the article in the home and it may stay lost for some time. Querent should cease any attempt to contact the family until a later date and that time should be carefully elected or planned.

FORTUNA — FIFTH HOUSE

BASIC

Brings a great sensitivity to the new and creative fields of art, drama, literature, invention, music and the personal abilities along these lines. A very active romantic and love life (as differentiated from just plain sex). If unafflicted, brings great luck in speculation, fulfillment of heart's desires and with children. Winning at games of chance. This position indicates an easygoing but powerful personality because this is the Sun's natural house and the Sun and Moon must be in near-time aspect to place Fortuna here. Early education fits this native well for coping with life's problems, thus minimizing them. Emotional release comes through friends, other people's children, social organizations and/or astrology.

CONSTRUCTIVE

Brings the inclination to use the creative abilities for the benefit of self, others and the public in general. Gives and receives help from younger people, especially their own children. There is the possibility of embarrassment through a chlid, but this can be handled humorously and openly, never secretly. The natives can back educational efforts with their personal endeavors in theatres, movies, television, uplifting lectures and schools. Can be a professional athlete or involved in a big and creative business...or both.

DESTRUCTIVE

Loss of energies through dissipation, self-indulgences, sexual intrigue or other types of speculation. Self-centered, gambling recklessly, headstrong, didactic and living the illusion of being a grand lord or lady. Being or having the reputation of being a prostitute, pimp or gigolo. Living in the fantasies of "only doing this until some big producer discovers me"...?

MATERIAL

Brings a liking for adventurous enterprises. May make money in catering to the needs of children and/or the entertainment public; manufacturing film, stage props, lights or toys, visual aids for education, etc. Luck in speculation, lotteries or gambling through theatrical ventures. This position is fortunate for scenic and costume designers and builders. Gains through children, love affairs and other non-concrete, speculative ventures.

SPIRITUAL

The creative and ceremonial side of spirituality is accented here. Must be careful not to become so spear-it-you-all, that it becomes a form of escapism. Should avoid wasting *too much* money on themselves and their selfish pleasures...even if that pleasure is giving to others. Try to develop a keen sense of what is *really* important and worthwhile in life. Can gain pleasure and experience in endowing schools, orphanages, municipal theatres and other things where there is little chance of monetary return.

HORARY

If unafflicted, the querent is not really deeply involved in the question. This must be handled very carefully, as *this* reading will make the difference between the querent's ever visiting another astrologer or not. Be honest, tell them that they already have the problem under control or, that it is not really a problem (read the rest of the chart too!!), and to continue along the path they are following. If afflicted, this can be one of the most severe of emotional problems. Study the *whole chart* very carefully before you answer, as you are probably the querent's last ditch effort. Know that the querent will follow your advice *to the letter!*

FORTUNA — SIXTH HOUSE

BASIC

Brings much interest in public welfare through both employment conditions and the health of the masses. There is a strong desire to be of service to the community; doing "relevant" things to institute progress and improvements. Discriminating, efficient and piercing intellect. Good digestion and assimilation of food intake. If afflicted, will bring many job changes, employment problems and health problems as indicated by the rest of the chart. Natives could deal with people in uniform, or be in uniform at some time in the life, which will be remembered as a good or fortunate experience. The emotional release will be through working with confined people, like prisoners, invalids, monks, nuns or those from other institutions. Activities of emotional release could be through painting, sculpture, writing, poetry, music, imaginative fiction or spiritual studies.

CONSTRUCTIVE

Involves the natives in seeking out the injustices of life and voluntarily devoting themselves to the causes of reformation. Beneficial sacrifice in serving those who are enslaved or they may work for worthy health and food reforms or sanitation projects. Pleasure and profit can be made from small animals. There can be a drive to help other people with their problems. This can be the common man who rises to fame (if chart is strong); the union official or politician who captures the imagination of the working class, like Hughey Long.

DESTRUCTIVE

Brings difficulties through, because of or to a subordinate. The desire to want to do everything alone can result in losses through illness or incapacity. There can be a near-sinister desire to resist change on the grounds that *they* can't see the benefit. A tendency to nose into and gossip about other people's affairs. These are the ones who are always pointing the finger at other people as a means of drawing attention away from their own shortcomings. The destructive emotional outlet can take the form of clandestine affairs and the use of drugs.

MATERIAL

Natives have near-magical abilities with labor and service to others as a means of making money for themselves. Could be a paid union organizer or a speculator in commodities (see Fortunes for Crop Prognostication). If in a service, especially where a uniform of some kind is worn to mark the vocation, they can rise rapidly into the higher officer's position. If in business, could have success working with or for the army or navy. There is a great love of pets, which can help them in becoming one of the best of veterinarians. With the proper education, the fields of doctor, nurse or surgeon should be within easy access. If afflicted, they may do much work for nothing, not even personal satisfaction.

SPIRITUAL

This is the position of testing intelligent understanding and reason (not intellect or logic: that's third house) of all spiritual laws the native learned, then applying them to serve the masses to the best of the native's ability. They must not depend upon subordinates for assistance, even though they can delegate authority, the responsibility is all theirs, along with the rewards. There should be a kind of losing of self in service to others, which will actually help the health and vitality. If afflicted, can indicate native may direct spiritual confidence games and charlatanism against the masses. This type of spiritual selfishness can be the cause of chronic ailments.

HORARY

If unafflicted, the job or duty of the querents will progress with slow, sure steps which will insure security, but little excitement. The pet or small animal will be returned safely, in a well cared for condition. If afflicted, the job problems can be overcome by the querents working in harmony with others and not being so set in their own ways. The animal, if returned, will need a check-up... Offering a reward could help!

FORTUNA — SEVENTH HOUSE

BASIC

Brings an interest in things of an idealistic nature; wanting to see only the good and beautiful in the law, justice, problems of marriage and divorce, war, international relations, contracts and even the public image the native's partners (by marriage, business or merely co-workers) make. The open public or others in general tend to become *the field* of activity. Success with contracts and the public at large, as long as they are trying to strike a balance. Concern with competition and competitors. Properly interpreted, this placement tells if relationships are of long or short duration, pleasant or unpleasant, meaningful or empty, cooperative or conflicting. For Fortuna to fall in the last degree of the sixth or early degree of the seventh, the Sun and Moon must be in near opposition; the rest of the chart will tell you if this is balance or pulling apart. Emotional release comes through the self, grooming, self-improvement, soul searching to create a better image and considerations which will, of course, attract a more desirable partner.

CONSTRUCTIVE

Benefits through cooperation, marriage, partnerships, yielding of egotism and selfishness for the benefit and interest of others. Help and assistance through law enforcement (material, mental or spiritual). Gain comes through joint efforts with others. Native's personality shines through harmonious relationships and partnerships. Long duration, pleasant and meaningful relationships are indicated here, if the self is seen as part of a greater whole. The natives will be relied upon to be the decisive one so long as they are considerate of the feelings and needs of others.

DESTRUCTIVE

Personal and marriage problems will interfere with the public expressions. Difficulties at/with or by the law (material, mental or spiritual). Lack of sympathy and understanding of/with or from partners in all categories. Plagued by threats of lawsuits. The natives could become the Public Enemies or open enemies to those they dislike, who are probably the very ones who are trying to help the native most. Brings short duration, argumentative and empty relationships. When relationships are established, personality conflicts, divorce or death will most likely end them. Disillusionment with others and with life itself. May create mental aberrations and finally seek psychiatric or other "mystic" help as the only salvation. Indecisive and unable to make up the mind before the time of action is past.

MATERIAL

Profit through bargains, luxury items and dealings with the law in any capacity. This may attract a wealthy partner (husband, wife or business associate). Money through dealings with the public or any cooperative effort. Needs a partner capable of great love (whatever level the partnership is on) for this native to function at peak efficiency.

SPIRITUAL

This brings the most difficult lessons imaginable; those of

learning how to receive as well as give. Must learn the joy of helping those in *need* of help and to distinguish between *need* and those who are merely too lazy to help themselves. This position must learn to forgive their enemies and even go the step farther of learning how to love them. This does not mean to take an enemy into the home or partnership. This love is given objectively in such a way that the enemies are not allowed to continue on their destructive path — with the native only.

HORARY

This placement is of benefit to the astrologer, if unafflicted. It signifies that the astrologer is truly the partner of the querent. It is of benefit to the querent, as they have a known and open helper and are not alone with the problem. The partner is not the enemy and is telling the truth. If badly afflicted, one the querent thinks of as a partner is really the source of the problem. Sometimes, just bringing this out in the open could bring a satisfactory conclusion to the problem. The partner is not telling the truth and *could* be the enemy (other indications agreeable) or the partner feels that the querent is not capable of accepting the truth!

FORTUNA — EIGHTH HOUSE

BASIC

Interest in the occult; legal matters of the partner's finances, resources or talents and abilities; private and public partnership resources and estates of the dead, which may be of value (real or sentimental) to the native. Good powers of regeneration and rejuvenation. Healthy sex life and good powers of visualization; not easy to fool or lie to. Excellent at research and investigation (in archives, as private-eye or top level diplomatic missions). A tremendous ability at keeping and remembering secrets. Emotional release comes through the native's own possessions, talents and abilities and through concentration on finding ingenious ways of earning finances and recognition by themselves.

CONSTRUCTIVE

Gain through partner's resourcers. An uncanny ability to make mutually beneficial contracts. One who can work with occult laws to the benefit of all concerned in an easy, natural and unaffected way. Honesty in handling the funds and resources of others (as executor of wills, confidential investor, etc.) A healthy and unshockable outlook on sex, no matter what others consider natural to themselves. The international diplomat, handling the secrets of nations. Very attractive, due to an aura of sexual magnetism and knowledge.

DESTRUCTIVE

Financial difficulties through the partner, brought on by laziness which makes the natives rely too much on the partner's resources and not enough on their own. Should avoid getting into unfamiliar physical, metaphysical or occult matters without top guidance from an *uninvolved* teacher. These destructive types *always* try to involve others in their own interests. If badly afflicted, these could be the thieves or black magicians who, through their ignorance, could destroy themselves and drag others with them. The ghoul, with a morbid fancy for death or the dead. The true perverts, forcing others into mental, physical or sexual acts not pleasant to them. The blackmailer, always digging into things others do not want known. The double agent or spy. Filled with erotic fantasies. Emotional blow-ups. Very attractive due to an aura of forbidden knowledge and sexiness.

MATERIAL

Could gain through dealing in occult items, services or momentos of the dead. The mortician with sensitivity and concern for the living. Profit from the talents and abilities of others, like a theatrical agency, trust funds, bequests, insurance companies or working for tax computation. Monies through inheritance. If afflicted, the inheritance will be contested. Could marry a reigning sovereign, business magnate, heir or heiress.

SPIRITUAL

Must control the emotions and desires to what is possible, without limiting possibility. Fantasy and day-dreaming need to be transmuted to constructive imagination and that transmuted into constructive action. Should learn to doubt the apparent and search for the inner meanings of life and death, events and things. This is a good placement for developing mediumship; the type of mediumship will be indicated by the aspects and the rest of the chart. Must not save for "rainy days" or old age, as it *will* be provided for. Should give to spiritual causes.

HORARY

If unafflicted, occult laws are at work to aid the querent. The legacy or settlement will be settled to the querent's benefit. If benefically aspected, the querents will receive much more than they hope for. The health will improve and the secrets will be made available to the querents. If afflicted, the laws are working for the other party and most likely the querents are trying to claim something they have no legal or occult right to.

FORTUNA — NINTH HOUSE

BASIC

Powerful urges and interests involving the depths of the studies of philosophy, religion and the higher laws. Development of the higher mind and education through distant travel. Attraction to wide dissemination of knowledge through publishing, exporting, importing or travel. Benefits through in-laws. For this placement the Sun and Moon must be in a near trine aspect, so at worst it is better than most other placements. Because of this being a cadent house, the native may tend to drift and be without drive for personal achievement. Emotional release is through concrete thought, communication and family or neighborhood involvement and often through the routine of daily living.

CONSTRUCTIVE

Comes through bringing peace, justice and understanding to others through unselfish visions and study. Benefits through/and from those at a distance. A jovial, not easily discouraged personality. Brings insights which help the self and others. Extremely philosophical and content to observe life and others in a detached manner of objectivity. Benefits come without much physical effort being expended; it's more of a mental labor and this is a labor of love.

DESTRUCTIVE

Love of gambling, misdirection of personal affections, misrepresentation, charlatanism, sacrificing others to personal and private gain and advancement. Morose and somber, with many impudent and impatient affections of "holier than thou." The prophets of doom and the manipulators of visions, who never seem to follow their own pronouncements. Inactivity which demands that "the world owes me and until I get it, I'm not going to do anything for anybody"... In short, mentally, physically and spiritually a lazy parasite.

MATERIAL

Gain through religious and philosophical publications and/or writing of higher thoughts to uplift the collective mind of mankind. Profit from long trips, outdoor activities and dealings with foreign countries. Association with any branch of the publishing field. Work with relatives through marriage. Dealings with the stock market, anything that will widen the field of endeavor and vision. As the consciousness expands, so will the money and earning power.

SPIRITUAL

This is the natural seer or clairvoyant. They will discover early in life that they have a direct line to the powers that be, as they experience direct and immediate answers to prayer in times of emergency. As with all good placements, the natives must be aware and not take these benefits for granted or (in ignorance) use them as a form of escapism. They must use these gifts in helping others, for whom these talents are not natural, to open their own awareness. The attitude of "I do it, why can't you?" is common here. Higher understanding must be developed to answer this and other "logical" questions, which by no means are true or realistic. The reality which must be discovered is that the *truly higher minded* are the servant of all!

HORARY

If unafflicted, brings benefits through the law or legal machinery. Fortune is in an unexpected turn of events and will bring off the querents' purpose, as long as they hold to good and high motives. Whether afflicted or unafflicted, the querents are not too deeply upset with this question. It is annoying to them and they have probably brooded over it for some time, in a moral or philosophical way, before deciding to turn it over to an astrologer. If unafflicted, the querents can be drawn out so they will uncover the full and complete answer, which lies just beneath their awareness level. If afflicted, the querents do not like what lies there. They harbor a fear that the answer they want may be immoral, vile or a sin, so you will have to word your answer very carefully. Show up the higher side of mental and/or spiritual gain possible through deprivation of the matter. In other words, things won't work out to their desires but there is gain (Jupiter's house and Sun and Moon in near trine) through the lessons to be learned; but you must always give them the consolation prize.

FORTUNA — TENTH HOUSE

BASIC

Sensitivity to personal or national governmental conditions, an interest in politics and a close feeling of public trends. Much luck connected with being in the right place at the right time. A serious and somewhat reserved personality. This is possibly the most important position of all, as it is the result of a near Sun-Moon square, falling in the house of recognition and public standing, creates ambition in the native. Success and its responsibilities are the golden dreams of fulfillment with this placement. According to the aspects, it brings a career (as opposed to a job), publicity and recognition, relationships with the status parent, employer, etc. Marriage or close relations with an older person of importance or wealth. Can be a basic conflict of the inner natures of the native. Career oriented, as the person is, success or failure is a matter of public record. Emotional release or polarization is through the home, family, basic security symbols, the factors of heredity and early foundations. In later life it can become a concern for the public.

CONSTRUCTIVE

This Moon square Sun placement goads the person into action and accomplishment, creating a self-made man or woman. They are usually popular because of their unselfishness and their attachment to the needs of humanity. Parent-employer relations are something that they pride themselves on. The ability to see through appearances and into the unlimited possibilities of anything they focus on is a basic talent. They can even find a useful application for failure or error, which they turn into an asset. This native is not afraid of work and effort when there is a goal to be achieved. Great executive ability and a true concern for those under them. They can always command wealth to back up any sincere endeavor. If afflicted, they could have the reputation for owning more valuables than they really have, so they could be hounded by get-rich-quick schemers.

DESTRUCTIVE

Brings a great talent for offending those in power socially, politically and occupationally. Misdirection of the personal following, like intentionally advising people into bad investments, painting lovely pictures of the glory of bankruptcy, etc., as a means of triumphing over them. Inability to hold onto gains, due to selfishness and egotism. Self-seeking, they always know everything better than the parent-employer. Start campaigns that show off *their* superiority, which gets them fired from the job; or they constantly quit jobs because of the "intolerable" conditions, which are "beneath" their status to adjust to. This is the get-rich-quick schemer, especially working older people, the gigolo, gold-digger or hustler. They put much work and effort into their schemes and are patient for the pay-off, but are usually found out (10th house) before the pay-off pays. There is a great display of wealth and affluence, all the way from name-dropping to quoting the price of everything they own, thus becoming a perfect set-up for robbery and con-games.

MATERIAL

Profit through large corporations and organizations, the individual career, community affairs and business. Marriage (and love too) to an older and financially secure person. In case of divorce, the native would be well taken care of. Planning methods and setting up the proper conditions to aid the elderly, rentals, land development or farming. Developing or creating empires out of common materials or waste. These natives will benefit by not following the family trade but by going against home conditions and customs and finding their own level and expression.

SPIRITUAL

Must avoid ostentatious displays of wealth, jewelry, land, furnishing and garb. Gain of spiritual purpose by backing welfare enterprises with work and money. If afflicted, pride will most likely bring on the necessary fall. If humility is learned through this, the spiritual progress will be a generous reward. These natives may have to renounce the quiet, meditative life and take an active part in the carnal world around them, even accepting the responsibility of fame and fortune, in order to achieve their spiritual goals, which are very high and multidimensional.

HORARY

In fixed signs stay with the job you now have, as it is secure and you would lose greatly by a change at this time. In cardinal signs there is great benefit in a change of position. If unafflicted, the querents should proceed with the project as planned, because the motives are of a superior nature. If afflicted, the querents are trying to force their will on others and are in line for a rude awakening, which could even include public scandal. Generally, and in mutable signs, a better job or position is in the offing. If the sign ruler is not badly aspected by the Sun (for a man) or the Moon (for a woman), the work will be subject to environmental conditions which the querents are trying to get away from. The higher salary is their only gain.

FORTUNA — ELEVENTH HOUSE

BASIC

This position accents friendships, teen relationships, hopes, aspirations and income through the profession. Profit through social contacts, close friends and developing the native's own personality. The personality is probably not socially inclined, but its objectivity and fairness makes it one of the native's greatest assets. Really big, personal dreams could come true with this placement. There is a desire to see and acquire better conditions for the community and humanity through the avenues of science, astrology and new age thought. Basically, this is not a materialistic placement but the indicator of the dreamer and planner who is not afraid to take a long shot that others would fear. It's not unusual for this audacity to pay off in a big way. The natives are not really concerned about this but it gives them backing for the next skyrocket. Emotional release comes through creative activities, educational pursuits, helping children and love affairs...in that order?

CONSTRUCTIVE

There is an uncanny ability to foresee and plan future results from present causes, in connection with mass movements and feelings. Gains through devoting the life and talents to the advancement of the Race of Man, thinking and working with unselfish sacrifice for the brotherhood of all. Gain through tackling the "impossible" dreams of self and others, which will benefit society as a whole. Can manipulate the basic potentials of experience to open avenues of advanced vision, thereby creating channels for long-range projects. This is the strong and silent guiding hand from behind the scenes. Very good placement for accurate prophecy of all types.

DESTRUCTIVE

Brings a narrow circle of friends, centering on private, selfish and self-indulgent ends. Uses abilities for personal gain, power and control. These are the evil prime ministers of affairs, wanting love and adoration but settling for fear and blind obedience, as they direct others into destructive channels. The grasping, power hungry individuals who want humanity to serve only them. If just *one* of their self-indulgences is lost to them, they cry and scream about their great sacrifices. They can be the devious behind-the-scene instigator of dispute, unrest and intrigue and are hypercritical know-it-alls...after the fact of course.

MATERIAL

This position is extremely good for income from the native's profession (no, not their job), gain through matters relating to society as a whole, social contacts and improvements in anything of a humanitarian nature. An indication of many wealthy friends on whom the native can depend for assistance in ventures. Good for fund raisers. Financial gain through secret or fraternal organizations. If badly afflicted the native will still get help from friends (Sun-Moon must be in near sextile for this placement) but they may exact a heavy price or high interest rates and the native could feel as though these obligations were a millstone around his neck.

SPIRITUAL

This placement teaches the native to be the friend of *all*. They must learn the value of friends for their individuality and uniqueness, not for what can be gained from them. The hopes and wishes should be aimed at spiritual achievement and progress which, if worked at, will take care of the material needs with little or no effort, depending on the native's sincerity. Happiness will be found in helping the partner's children or in creative efforts and promoting brotherly relations with all.

HORARY

If unafflicted, help will come through social alliances, civic organizations or friends. The aspirations are well founded and opportunity for successful conclusion is open through working harmoniously along the lines indicated. Legislation is in the querents' favor. Be honest and straightforward, with no smugness or arrogance. If badly afflicted, the querents are trying to go against the tides of the matter. They should seek a benefit through cooperation. If a being is missing, check the legs upon return, which will happen after many false leads and delays.

FORTUNA — TWELFTH HOUSE

BASIC

In this house of frustration and non-fulfillment, Fortuna can feel limited to a serious extent. There is a restless and almost romantic fatalism and curiosity about distant places, the sea, mysterious locals and danger. These feelings can be honed into a highly constructive imagination or prophetic sense, which the native can use to great advantage. The native finds the thanks and obligation of others to be an embarrrassment. The native's product, rather than the personality, is accented here. Concentration and service (both mental and physical) for the aid of the majority is of great benefit to the native. Truly, nothing can be hidden from these natives; but a lot depends upon their ability to understand and *accept* themselves on their own ground and not on the average "norm" of society. Dreams can often bring the keys to material, social and business concerns. These natives have an almost physical reaction to the deeper trends of events or the "skeins of fate". This is just one of the hints of the native's mediumistic consciousness. There is a personal detachment even with their own affairs. Emotional release is through employment conditions, health, pets and the mate's inhibitions.

CONSTRUCTIVE

Benefit and gain through secluded work, as in archives, monasteries, prisons, hospitals and other sequestered institutions. If other indications concur, employment in films and television is indicated, where the fine flair for fantasy, mysticism and illusion is of great asset. The circus is also open to these natives if Fortuna is well aspected. Care must be taken as to where monies are banked or invested. If afflicted, the native could lose through bank failures, etc. If well aspected, gain is possible through bank failures. There is a keen sense of awareness of the undercurrents in all affairs, which can keep the natives ahead of any project they're involved with in any way.

DESTRUCTIVE

There is a tendency to withdraw from open and active participation in life or affairs. There can be a demanding that others prove their good will, while the natives withhold theirs. They are prone to spying, indulging in intrigue and behind-the-scenes manipultion of a heedless and destructive nature. With their extreme patience and self-sacrifice, they can hatch, plan and carry out diabolical schemes on a global scale, taking over governments, instigating wars, religious and national pride and envy, while outwardly remaining the "nice little family next door." These are the satanic messiahs, cast by "fate" into the role of dark saviours. On the lower levels, these are the blood-rite occultists; the hypnotists who exhort their subjects to ludicrous and embarrassing acts; the mystical charlatans and the suicide-bent hypochondriacs who drain others of their energies through the so called sympathy they inspire.

MATERIAL

Ready cash can be seriously tied up, attached, promised, confiscated or proven to be purely hypothetical. The natives must learn early in life not to count on anything that they do not have *complete* control of personally. Avenues of long range employment are psychology, parapsychology, caring for the rehabilitation of alcoholic or narcotic addicts, art, photography, any line of work which tries to expand mankind's horizons, to bringing the unknown into the realm of reliable tools. Abraham Lincoln had this placement. His detached attitude was a positive tool which helped America and others see the bigger panorama of life.

SPIRITUAL

The natives have a strong desire to divest themselves of all worldly goods and to give to the poor. They should cultivate a kindly spirit but not get carried to the extremes of needing material charity themselves. They must develop scrupulous honesty in all intentions, as a guideline to their own behaviour. They have natural mediumship abilities but that is not enough. The native must develop and understand these abilities and bring them under conscious control so they are always aware of the motive behind their use. These people derive the greatest pleasure and satisfaction from giving silently and anonymously.

HORARY

If well aspected, the querents must rely on their own inner resources to resolve the problem. The lost item is in the home. The querents themselves put it in a so-called safe and secret place. If there are only one or two afflictions, the article was taken by a secret enemy who is very familiar with the object. Things will go easier for the querents if they will try to adjust to society and/or the others involved by the question. They must put themselves in the other person's shoes. If heavily afflicted, the querents do not want to adjust to the situation or society. Sometimes they cannot, due to personal afflictions like blindness, broken bones, etc. The lost item is beyond recall or destroyed. The lost person could be in an institution or comatose in a hospital.

This is an outline of how to read Fortuna in the houses. Use every scrap of knowledge you have. If you are in doubt about what rules or has affinity to what, check Rex Bill's *The Rulership Book*. The houses, like the Fortunes, are mundane divisions. The house placement is the most important thing, as far as the Fortunes are concerned. This tells what department of life will be stimulated

when the particular Fortune is agitated. The signs are qualifying indicators, which are the shades of temperament likely to be expressed
by the agitated Fortune.

I will give (in less detail) just a few more of the Fortunes
through the houses so you can use them as a guideline for developing your own interpretations.

THE PART OF SPIRIT (#2)

SPIRIT—FIRST HOUSE

The basic morale or spirit of life depends on how well the
natives are able to center their achievements in their own personality
and dramatize themselves as a unique symbol to others. Their
satisfaction comes through self-possession rather than any exter-
nalized manifestations. It is possible to become so engrossed in the
self that they are not aware when others begin to ignore them; by the
same token, they shouldn't allow themselves to become suspicious
of the motives of others or they could develop a persecution complex. For these people a full life lies in becoming their own true and
individual selves.

SPIRIT — SECOND HOUSE

The fundamental pleasure or spirit in life hinges on the degree
that personal success can inspire a greater success and striving for
accomplishment in others or in being part of a plan of success.
These are the people who would die spiritually if they were made to
rest on their laurels. To them success is not an end in itself, but a
spiritual renewal of spiritual fact and manifestation. The full life is
one which is constantly busy, hurdling obstacles for the self and
others, finding the thrill of looking forward to an optimistic tomorrow in the middle of a pessimistic today.

SPIRIT — THIRD HOUSE

The gift of life for these natives' spirit lies in their ability to find
a use and purpose for everything in their environment. Their back-
up comes from the way the world agrees with them (their Fortuna
must be in the tenth house) after they have learned to assert
themselves in their profession. The rich life is theirs as they discover
how to blend their creative interests and all the details of life into a

picture of the whole, rather than restrict themselves to one point of view.

SPIRIT — FOURTH HOUSE

The fundamental pleasure of spirit is based in seeing the grassroots realities, the unchangeable constants and the ever-dependable eternals that underlie the illusion of change. These natives must discover a central theme in life, a central point of desire and accomplishment or they will not really get started. Satisfaction comes from recognizing and expressing the values of human effort and growth.

SPIRIT — FIFTH HOUSE

This creative theme of spirit lies in being able to see another's idea, concept or viewpoint and adapting it to the native's expression or any person or movement who needs it. From this position can be seen the wider application of every thought. The natives' satisfaction lies in catching the better impulse in others, matching it themselves and encouraring an easy camaraderie of higher precepts still. Their ideal of success is in acting as an agent for others, with a free-flowing vitality that can be ingenuous without becoming vulgar.

SPIRIT — SIXTH HOUSE

These natives' spirit lies in the satisfaction of labor well done, the exhilarating exaltation (physical, mental, emotional or spiritual) of the act itself rather than just achievement of results and completion. Their thrill of satisfaction comes when they are called upon to make adjustments and decisions in times of need; the joyous humility when others rely on them to rise to the occasion.

SPIRIT — SEVENTH HOUSE

Here the spiritual pleasure in life is in meeting each and every issue of life face to face, approaching it on its own unique and peculiar terms. These natives' triumph is in learning how to leave their own preconceptions and prejudices at home and how to take advantage of even chance inconveniences for their own growth and experience. The riches of life are funneled to them through the uncertainty of external conditions and affairs, which makes them rely on their genius in applying their underlying capabilities.

SPIRIT — EIGHTH HOUSE

These people's spiritual bloom comes with the appreciation of their own growth through the richness of personality, which may or may not ever gain them acclaim. While often indolent, they rapidly arise to any outside stimulus of wrong-doing and successfully overcome all opposition, luxuriating in the assurance of regeneration it brings them. Greater satisfaction comes through their own efforts of self-discipline, which uncovers the illimitable resources of a creative personality.

SPIRIT — NINTH HOUSE

Their spiritual thrill is in their ability to generalize experience for themselves and others and then finding its specific application to each unique situation. This brings the native a sense of the world of man, life and God as one homogeneous whole, not made of little sections glued together, but truly an interdependent and self-sustaining unit. For them Shangri-la is gained through expanding the concepts of the mind so they can remold their world from any starting point.

SPIRIT — TENTH HOUSE

This morale of spirit depends on the recognition the natives receive from others, be it that they are only sensitive to the expectations of others or truly sensitive to the needs and real nature of everything around them. Satisfaction comes in the degree that their efforts are a contribution to the community in which they circulate. They don't have to be in command, but they must know that their contributions are an important factor to the flow of events and activity, along the line of the highest hopes of all concerned.

SPIRIT — ELEVENTH HOUSE

These natives' spiritual assurance is dependent on the strengthened continuity of their optimism, which tells them that the best part of life lies ahead and the present is only a gateway to tomorrow's blessings. Their satisfaction grows in their simple but idealistic set of temperament, which depends upon cultivating their own personal resources. A great capacity for give and take makes life a dynamic experience and adventure.

SPIRIT — TWELFTH HOUSE

The fundamental morale of spirit depends on the privacy and self-sufficiency of the native's inner motivations. They are a law unto themselves (for good or bad) and they make and maintain their own individual basis of value. Satisfaction arises from the experiences of their own integrity. These people are only happy when they remain true to their own inner selves in every way, without compromise to the demands of others or the life around them.

THE PART OF LIFE: REINCARNATION (#8)

LIFE — FIRST HOUSE

The native's best effort of self-awareness in life comes through spontaneity. They make no attempt to conform to ideas which do not correspond to their inner compulsions, and are not pushed or cajoled into action until the inner guard gives an unqualified "yes". Otherwise observe and catalogue, so they can always base their action on the maximum amount of fact. They must learn to use facts as a socially acceptable excuse to follow their own inner drives. The soul drive is to establish their individuality as a channel for the inherent potentialities of the world around them. They can get the support of others, if their aims are based in their soul drive.

LIFE — SECOND HOUSE

Their dynamics of self-fulfillment lie in not frittering away their talents. They should do nothing unless they can wholeheartedly bring all of their personal resources into its accomplishment. These natives must use everything that touches them deeply and learn to make a living reality of the powers of manifestation out of all ties of love and obligation. They gain most when they don't stop to weigh the personal advantages of their actions. They have a generosity of soul that finds happiness through distinguishing between wastefulness and fellowship.

LIFE — THIRD HOUSE

Here the natives' road to self-understanding needs a healthy attitude toward their environment and working spontaneously with those around them. They display their active best when they play down all hesitation and uncertainty within themselves, because, for their soul, this life is a testing ground which demands that they learn decisive action. The direction is not pointed out or circumscribed, so long as they do not go against their inner wishes. In this life, the whole world is their workshop. Cooperation is found insofar as they are true to their own deeper objectives.

LIFE — FOURTH HOUSE

This native's path of self-unfoldment needs a concept of the self in relationship to eternal values. "Unto thine own (natural) self, be true," applies here more than in any other placement, because they are at their best advantage as they learn to accept responsibility for the ideals demanded of them by others. Here the soul urge wearies of petty things; so if they would find contentment, they must turn to deeper and more eternal realities. Otherwise they may find themselves running frantically from one fad or thrill to another, without ever finding satisfaction, as life and advancement seem to pass them by. The development of spiritual stability of character is the quality that makes the difference.

LIFE — FIFTH HOUSE

Here is the goal of self-realization which depends on the unleashing of the native's inner irrepressible spontaneity of action, when it is channeled in a bubbling and natural way to stimulate the real self-expression of others. Their best action comes from centering their life around the development and refinement of their own creative gifts. This soul is basically carefree and they must learn to share this quality in a way that inspires and encourages others to be more optimistic of their own capabilities. Success in any area of life depends on the purity of their free spiritual spontaneity to develop their own creative talents.

LIFE — SIXTH HOUSE

Here the basic drive for self-expression needs enduring social contacts with others. These natives are at their delightful best when bringing order out of chaos and reconciling differences of the human relationships. Life becomes more valuable to the extent they are able to help others discover themselves spiritually, psychologically or in taking the responsibility for the administration of their own affairs. The actions of these natives are at their best advantage when they emphasize the joy of doing above the remote or ultimate objective. These natives can find a welcome place among people anywhere, when they truly desire to call forth the best expressions of others' spiritual energies.

LIFE — SEVENTH HOUSE

The drive for self-appreciation demands that these natives find causes they can pour their energies into, or locate individuals of special potential and promise whom they can work cooperatively with. They shine forth in the best light when they can associate with realities that are larger than their own personality. Their best action is based on their ability to be objective about their inner ideas and ideals and to balance their concern for others with concern for self. Their soul demands an inner spiritual justification for its existence. Without this, the life experience turns in upon itself, imprisoning the soul urge in a kind of limbo. They *must* know that life has something more to it than just an animal existence.

LIFE — EIGHTH HOUSE

The need for self-gratification depends upon the native's ability to constantly reconstruct their own life so they can always be the embodiment of a person of consequence to others. Their best effort is called forth as they discover the inner hunger of human hearts and rush to answer that call, with sensitivities alert to discover all the possibilities in others. This soul is extremely susceptible to external pressures and influences, so they must make sure that they respond only to the highest, not the lowest. They are capable of both! These natives can sway people easily to their visions. Make sure they are for the good of humanity and not just the self; because whatever they are capable of commanding by their magnetism becomes their responsibility.

LIFE — NINTH HOUSE

The natives' adventures of self-discovery need their willingness to take responsibility for their own attitudes and states of mind. They begin to radiate as they give expression only to their higher impulses, which cannot deny a constant contact with eternal realities. The life becomes meaningful and easy as they manifest their own ideals rather than react to outside pressures and events. Their actions are at their best advantage when they try, by example, to persuade others to stand side by side with them. They must *never* demand or coerce. Here the soul is extremely sensitive to spiritual values, so doubt of self and indecision in matters of importance must be discouraged. They should seek the spiritual roots of all matters and go forward with a hymn in their heart. They can win the world to their cause if they are patient and understanding and build on their spiritual insights, as life and experience unfolds them.

LIFE — TENTH HOUSE

The solidity of self-establishment is founded on the native's willingness to stand by themselves before all mankind and take the applause and sneers for their inner beliefs and ideals. They shine as they learn to commit themselves wholeheartedly, spontaneously and without vacillation when decision and command are needed. Their best advantage of action manifests as they become spiritually sure of themselves. They will do better as they develop decisiveness, even though at first it may lead to embarrassing mistakes. The soul demands the right to forge its own way because it knows its goals in life. These goals are rooted in the spiritual significance of individual responsibility, making the whole life-drama subservient to the inner self-establishment of the soul.

LIFE — ELEVENTH HOUSE

Here the native's consciousness of self-expansion needs the response of encouragement received from others as well as from itself, along with a keen assessment of incoming material. They are at their best as they exercise their phenomenal ability to recognize the hidden potentials of all people and things. The actions are most advantageous when founded on brotherly love for the Universe as a whole, not just mankind. These natives' soul-vision is very high indeed; and if events are to have any meaning for them, they will have to direct their insights into every phase of their development. They can dwell in a wonderland of spiritual realities, which will bring an adventuresome excitement and encouragement from every phase and action of existence.

LIFE — TWELFTH HOUSE

This path of self-attunement uses every latent sensitivity of the normally unsuspected possibilities of every experience in life. These natives are at their best as they discover how to ritualize and symbolize the life experience. This is necessary simply because of the huge amount of data and insight they are able to extract from any given situation. They gain their maximum advantage as they learn how to trace the motivating undercurrents of things and actions and interpret these deeper meanings to others. When it comes to self-renewal, their soul is so untiring that it is a source of constant comfort to near ones. It is also a very disturbing influence to those who are unbalanced within. When they depend on the invisible support of soul to strengthen them they are capable of unraveling and revealing the whole meaning of life.

*   *   *

Now, reread these delineations until you see how the identifying symbolism of the name of the Fortune has been blended with the varied meanings of each house to supply the multi-leveled reading I have given for Fortuna or the capsulized paragraph given for Spirit and Life.

The house placement for the Fortune is the strongest influence for interpretation because both houses and Fortunes are mundane concepts. Houses signify departments of life experiences and activities. The Fortunes like the planets, read truer to the house they are in, the nearer they approach the true center of the house. The nearer they are to the cusp, the more you must consider a blending of that preceding or succeeding house.

Intercepted signs have little effect on the interpretation of the Fortunes, except to make their sensitive reactions less obvious on the material-social level. The influence will still be there when aspected or touched off. The outer manifestation will just not be easily discernible. Insensitive people may not notice it at all, while the extremely sensitive will react to it as violently as a physical blow.

The second most important consideration necessary for accurate reading of the Fortunes are the aspects. An evil aspect from Saturn, for instance, can wipe out any beneficial effect of a Fortune, By the same token, the Part of Perversion can be made unmanifest in this same manner. Our terms of good and evil, benefic and malefic leave much to be desired on the level of ordinary understanding in that a malefic aspect from an evil planet can destroy a debilitating perversion. Perhaps this is what is meant in the old astrological texts by the term *transmutation of energies.*

Since the Fortunes are only sensitive points and have no action of their own, the aspects are the activating agents, by progression, direction and/or transit. Conjunction and opposition are the strongest activating aspects of the Fortunes. The square, trine or sextile are fairly weak activators, but must be considered as qualifiers if a Fortune is struck by an opposition or conjunction at the same time it is receiving a square, trine or sextile. The minor aspects are almost non-existent as activators, unless the Fortune is aspected by three or more minor aspects *at the same time.*

As with everything else in astrology, when reading the aspects to the Fortunes you must consider the whole chart in order to know if the people are likely to use an opposition as a balancing agent or a pulling apart, if they will use a conjunction as a conjoined aid or intrusion, etc. For special interpretations of aspects, read James Raymond Wolfe's article "Your Horoscope According to the Ancients" in the June 1970 issue of *Astrology, Your Daily Horoscope;* which should be available through any local astrological library.

For further delineations of the Fortunes themselves, look up the various references cited in the bibliography section of this book; the Marc Edmund Jones articles are especially recommended.

Chapter VI
FORTUNES IN
THE SIGNS

The signs, in association with the Fortunes, bring in descriptive coloration of the action indicated by the house placement and the activating spark of the aspects. The signs tint and mold the actions, pulling in little helps and hindrances within the greater influence of the house position.

FORTUNA IN THE SIGNS

FORTUNA — ARIES

Leads the natives to express their innovative and creative efforts through aggressive ideas, with which they meet life's obstacles, This *is* the sign of the Sun's exaltation. Between zero degrees of Aries and twenty degrees of Aries, the natives will attract increasing gain from their own efforts as they mature. If over twenty degrees of Aries the natives may find themselves attracting threats and catastrophes (of the nature of the house placement), which they can meet and overcome with those aggressive ideas. If these natives work in banking or speculation, this placement can be an aid to their advancement, unless the fifth house is afflicted or the Moon is badly aspected by or conjunct Mars or Uranus.

FORTUNA — TAURUS

This is a good sign for Fortuna, as it is the Moon's exaltation, signifying fortune through marriage or through an influence from the opposite sex. Many changes sweep these natives, (unless heavily afflicted) upward on the ladder of success, as indicated by the house position. In a woman's chart, she may even realize benefits from extra-marital affairs. Between ten and twenty degrees of Taurus there can be very trying financial periods, balanced by very successful ones, but always a tendency to splurge and live beyond the means. Difficult aspects from Mars, unless very carefully handled, can bring ruin to the difficult periods. From twenty degrees of Taurus on is the most unstable sector of this good sign. The natives are prone to giving the impression of greater wealth than they possess, inviting responsibilities they are incapable of meeting.

FORTUNA — GEMINI

Sucess in this sign is indicated by the individual's merit and intelligence, along the lines signified by the house placement. Relationships with near-relatives take on a major importance. Between ten and twenty degrees of Gemini, Fortuna signifies success which grows gradually. This can only be broken by the native's loss of self-confidence; even with this, a strong tenth house can stabilize the success and leave less room for self-doubt. The last ten degrees of Gemini fortifies Fortuna more than the rest of the sign, bringing the necessary self-assurance and dispursing of shadows, intrigue and worry.

FORTUNA — CANCER

Fortuna is well-signed here (the sign of the Moon's dignity). Opportunities and benefits are nicely balanced in this sign, especially if the Moon favorably aspects Fortuna. A conjunction of Moon-Fortuna in the angles seems to open the floodgates to Lady Luck, bringing success in *any* undertaking. Much financial success, as indicated by the house placement, and more than one benefit through the wife, husband or parents. From ten to twenty degrees of Cancer brings in a constant stirring of variety, change and/or travel around the picture of the native's success. From twenty degrees of Cancer on attracts rapid achievement, success and that eleventh hour help from unexpected sources which saves the native from catastrophic errors.

FORTUNA — LEO

With the Sun dignified in Leo, this placement brings a sense of self-assurance to the natives, helping them to rise to the highest indicated by Fortuna's house placement and to aspire to leadership in that field. The rise will appear to be due to lucky breaks; but in reality it's because these natives are not easily fooled by social illusions, so they can see and grasp opportunities of which others aren't even aware. From ten to twenty degrees of Leo favors gain through writing, publishing and speaking tours in all high minded and religious fields and a keen eye which can sort out falsehoods. From twenty degrees of Leo on indicates that the rise in position can create envy and many enemies. Often the enemies will create so many difficulties and obstacles that the natives must resort to violence or dictatorial tactics to settle them down.

FORTUNA — VIRGO

Directs success toward the intellectual pursuits of the house position indicated. An indication of possible wealth, but seldom philanthropy, probably because this native must adhere to strict economy to acquire anything of value. Success comes from paying attention to details, small things and enterprises of limited scope. From ten to twenty degrees of Virgo is not conducive to any long range stability, so the assets should be kept in a comparatively liquid state. From twenty degrees of Virgo on, the native can look forward to a rich and intellectually rewarding marriage, especially if Moon or Venus are in harmonious aspect.

FORTUNA — LIBRA

Natives are more interested in material gain than in marital love. Probably because of this, they are not afraid to *work* at a marriage of convenience until they make a beautiful semblance of "perfect wedded bliss." If promotions or sudden elevations of position come about through the marriage, isn't that fortunate? Usually, good and lasting health accompany this sign placement. From ten to twenty degrees of Libra brings results of a very high order, even without marriage, because of the extreme focus of intelligence. The happiness revolves more around noble sentiments and high ideals, so the native can attract many great honors. From twenty degrees of Libra on these natives can have an eternally youthful zest for life, overlaying a shy, childlike nature that never misses an offered advantage, which even forces their enemies to think of them warmly.

FORTUNA — SCORPIO

Favors ambition *if* the native is willing to work aggressively but quietly to win the goals of the house placement. When this Fortune smiles, the native seldom stops to ask if the deal is legitimate or not. Often friends and family feel they have to make excuses or apologies for the native's behavior, unless Fortuna is receiving good aspects from benefics. This is a good placement for hard-headed business ventures. From ten to twenty degrees of Scorpio indicates that the native will have good health and great physical resistance to disease. Sudden fortunes can be made and lost in the fields indicated by the house position. From twenty degrees of Scorpio on, the native can tend to get lazy and sponge off of family and friends or get involved in shady "get-rich-quick" deals. If afflicted by malefics, robbery and illegal speculation can be indicated.

FORTUNA — SAGITTARIUS

Attracts perservering work, integrity, personal organization and the tools to slowly but surely build security in the area indicated by the house placement. These natives could equip themselves for public office, college board-of-trustees member, publisher or in the ecclesiastical fields. In any event, they are certain to win the respect of superiors because they unconsciously guard the superior's reputation and security. From ten to twenty degrees of Sagittarius, with the aid of a good aspect from Jupiter, the native can win growing and lasting wealth without too much effort. From twenty degrees of Sagittarius on, if the native can blend it with the house position, fortune smiles from the areas of real estate, rental property, schools and theatrical ventures. Unfortunately, these people seem to fear loss and so seldom enjoy their gains.

FORTUNA — CAPRICORN

No one knows better than these natives that wealth does not bring happiness. They seldom lack money, but they worry and are filled with many anxieties about the future of the banking institutions, their stability and security. Therefore, you will find these people investing in stable commodities, real estate, gold mines or else wearing money belts from ankle to wrist. From ten to twenty degrees of Capricorn represents the person who lends at high rates and collects good dividends but who never really has any control over the flow. This is especially true if adversely aspected by Jupiter. With a good Jupiter aspect, the native could be a top-notch loan shark. From twenty degrees of Capricorn on, the natives should invest in long term plans that grow steadily and surely, such as life insurance, annuities and oil substitute research; because if the Sun is well aspected, they will live to a very ripe old age.

FORTUNA — AQUARIUS

These natives' uninvolved objectivity and sympathetic concern for others are traits that should prepare them for a future in big business, large projects and in undertakings subsidized by other people's money. They will be able to benefit without endangering their associates or others. From ten to twenty degrees Aquarius the native should not depend on income from legacies or wills from the female side of the family (including a wife). The native could also be a financial wastrel. From twenty degrees of Aquarius on, the ideals should be on a higher plane, according to the house position, with a very broad outlook and a certain nobility of purpose. A good aspect from Jupiter or Sun could elevate this person to a position of fame, wealth and high honors, in that order.

FORTUNA — PISCES

In this sign, the native should become familiar with the spiritual rewards indicated by the house placement. If there are good aspects the native can live in modest comfort, with little unexpected benefits from time to time. From ten to twenty degrees of Pisces prudence is indicated because if Sun and/or Moon are dignified in any manner and send out good aspects, the natives will live for a very long time; so preparation should be undertaken early in life. From twenty degrees of Pisces on, if Fortuna is in the angles, money will not be so difficult to come by and it could steadily increase. *Only* if Mars and/or the fifth house are powerful, can this native even consider gambling as a means of increasing his income.

Now reread these delineations until you see just how the key words for the signs have been blended with the name Fortuna or Success. Notice further how the keywords for the decanates have been blended in. If your expertise extends to the dwads, include them for more subtle reading. Next, in *your* interpretations, consider the dignity, detriment, exaltation and fall signs and degrees of the planets involved in the formula of the Fortune you are using. In this context reread Fortuna in Aries; "From zero degrees of Aries to twenty degrees of Aries, the natives will attract increasing gain from their own efforts as they mature." The Sun is involved in computing Fortuna; the Sun's exaltation degree is at nineteen Aries, so naturally things will get increasingly better as Fortuna approaches nineteen degrees of Aries.

Here is a list of rulerships and dignities that may help you delineate the various Fortunes in the signs:

ARIES: (Mars dignified; Venus detrimented)
0° to 9° ruled by Mars
10° to 19° ruled by Mars-Sun (Leo influence)
19° of Aries is the Sun's exaltation degree.
20° to 29° ruled by Mars-Jupiter (Sagittarius influence)
21° of Aries is Saturn's degree of fall.

TAURUS: (Venus dignified; Pluto detrimented)
0° to 9° ruled by Venus
3° of Taurus is the Moon's exaltation degree.
10° to 19° ruled by Venus-Mercury (Virgo influence)
15° of Taurus is Uranus' degree of fall.
20° to 29° ruled by Venus-Saturn (Capricorn influence)

GEMINI: (Mercury dignified; Jupiter detrimented)
0° to 9° ruled by Mercury
10° to 19° ruled by Mercury-Venus (Libra influence)
20° to 29° ruled by Mercury-Uranus (Aquarius influence)
(No exaltations or fall as yet have been discovered, although the North node of the Moon seems to be at its best at 3° Gemini)

CANCER: (Moon dignified; Saturn detrimented)
0° to 9° ruled by Moon
10° to 19° ruled by Moon-Pluto (Scorpio influence)
15° of Cancer is Jupiter's exaltation degree.
20° to 29° ruled by Moon-Neptune (Pisces influence)
28° of Cancer is Mars' degree of fall.

LEO: (Sun dignified; Uranus detrimented)
  0° to 9° ruled by Sun
  10° to 19° ruled by Sun-Jupiter (Sagittarius influence)
  19° of Leo is Neptune's exaltation degree.
  20° to 29° ruled by Sun-Mars (Aries influence)
  27° of Leo is Mercury's degree of fall.

VIRGO: (Mercury dignified; Neptune detrimented)
  0° to 9° ruled by Mercury
  10° to 19° ruled by Mercury-Saturn (Capricorn influence)
  15° of Virgo is Pluto's exaltation degree.
  20° to 29° ruled by Mercury-Venus (Taurus influence)
  27° of Virgo is Venus' degree of fall.

LIBRA: (Venus dignified; Mars detrimented)
  0° to 9° ruled by Venus
  10° to 19° ruled by Venus-Uranus (Aquarius influence)
  19° of Libra is the Sun's degree of fall.
  20° to 29° ruled by Venus-Mercury (Gemini influence)
  21° of Libra is Saturn's exaltation degree.

SCORPIO: (Pluto dignified; Venus detrimented)
  0° to 9° ruled by Pluto
  3° of Scorpio is the Moon's degree of fall.
  10° to 19° ruled by Pluto-Neptune (Pisces influence)
  15° of Scorpio is Uranus' exaltation degree.
  20° to 29° ruled by Pluto-Moon (Cancer influence)

SAGITTARIUS: (Jupiter dignified; Mercury detrimented)
  0° to 9° ruled by Jupiter
  10° to 19° ruled by Jupiter-Mars (Aries influence)
  20° to 29° ruled by Jupiter-Sun (Leo influence)
  (exaltations or fall as yet have been discovered, although the
  south node of the Moon seems to be at its best at 3°
  Sagittarius)

CAPRICORN: (Saturn dignified; Moon detrimented)
  0° to 9° ruled by Saturn
  10° to 19° ruled by Saturn-Venus (Taurus influence)
  15° of Capricorn is Jupiter's degree of fall.

20° to 29° ruled by Saturn-Mercury (Virgo influence)
28° of Capricorn is Mars' exaltation degree.

AQUARIUS: (Uranus dignified; Sun detrimented)
 0° to 9° ruled by Uranus
 10° to 19° ruled by Uranus-Mercury (Gemini influence)
 19° of Aquarius is Neptune's degree of fall.
 20° to 29° ruled by Uranus-Venus (Libra influence)
 27° of Aquarius is Mercury's exaltation degree.

PISCES: (Neptune dignified; Mercury detrimented)
 0° to 9° ruled by Neptune
 10° to 19° ruled by Neptune-Moon (Cancer influence)
 15° of Pisces is Pluto's degree of fall.
 20° to 29° ruled by Neptune-Pluto (Scorpio influence)
 27° of Pisces is Venus' exaltation degree.

I know that many will loudly decry my assignment of Pluto to
Scorpio and giving the exaltation of Mercury to Aquarius, among
other pet beliefs I have ignored. But remember that every book or
writing is that writer's opinion, to be accepted or rejected by the
reader as they will. When studying astrology, I found my teachers
arguing these and other points rather heatedly. They often backed
up their beliefs with "...but so and so says...", as though so and
so were the ultimate authority. In my investigation I have tried to
depend solely on observation and the histories of the lives of the
people whose charts I used. To find Pluto in Aries and Scorpio, I
worked with historical charts of those people whose life is a matter
of record. Here the problem was different. Around these lives the
mythos and charm of the long-dead were already entwined. It took
much digging to get first hand accounts that made them into real
people and not larger-than-life gods or demons. Where you question my findings, check them out for yourself.

My opinion is another matter. I assign Virgo's rulership to the
unverified planet Vulcan. Vulcan was the craftsman of the gods, the
tireless servant to the gods' tastes for intricate creations of the
earth's metals. Whoever heard of Mercury's giving willing service
with no practical jokes or a laugh at someone else's expense? To
Taurus, I would assign a slower moving planet than Venus, perhaps

Bacchus, the much touted trans-Pluto planet. I would like to have it
called Pan, when and if the planet is verified. Pan was the son of
Venus. So why shouldn't "mamma" protect his sign until he
returns? Sudden frights are still called pan-ics. And what happens
when Taurus has had all it can take and finally blows its stack? The
Moon is exalted in Taurus...and so was Selene (the Moon God-
dess) when Pan seduced her in the guise of a glowing white ram.
Whoever heard of Taurus' planning and scheming to get even with
someone? That's Libra. That's Venus. Taurus is too much in love
with good company and the bountiful manifestations of earth,
which was Pan's domain. Taurus loves the smell of clean air,
natural earth odors and flowers in bloom, not the synthetic
cosmetics and the unnaturally sweetened tastes of Venus.

Futhermore, it is my *belief* that mythologies are histories of actual events, recorded in the only consistent dating system that is
always discernible regardless of any culture's calendar. That constant calendar is astrology. To date mythological events it is only
necessary to take a composite mythology of the ancient gods
(planets) and run your computers back to see when everything lined
up in those shapes (signs). Was earth ever destroyed by flood
waters? When did Jupiter, in the guise of a bull (Taurus) supposedly
"rape" Europa? What was Saturn's reaction (sign it was in)? What
were the reactions (signs) of Venus, Mars, Mercury? Add all of
these together and you may have an accurate method of dating the
flood which is not dependent on A.D. or B.C. or any other man-
made calendar. But, these are my own pet beliefs and opinions. You
are certainly entitled to yours.

Chapter VII
FORTUNA IN
WRECK-TIFICATION

To my knowledge there are really no sure and positive methods of rectification that always give one hundred percent satisfaction. There are methods that satisfy the various schools and branches of astrological thought; but there are none that satisfy *all* schools and branches of astrological thought.

Into this melee I have decided to throw my "quickie" method, by the use of Fortuna in the chart.

When I am in serious doubt as to a birth time, I usually start the delineation by interpreting Fortuna and stating: "If the chart is correct, you should have had some sudden changes of fortune on such and such a date." (especially if I can find a good hit or opposition of Uranus in the native's lifetime). This brazen approach serves two purposes: (1) it tells me if the birth minute is accurate; and (2) by my bringing a statement like that out of apparently nowhere, the person literally hangs on to every word I say after that and I have gained their utmost cooperation.

If I am off by a year or so, I can quickly pencil in the variation in degrees around the wheel (which I make no effort to hide). They can see that their correction of my reading has made me reconsider my calculations. In this case they realize that we are really partners in this interpretation of their chart, and they become as relaxed as an old friend. Then I'll throw out another delineation of another

Fortune (recalculated by my "quickie" method). With the altera-
tion, this one usually hits dead on.

Fortuna moves at the near mean average of one degree, three
minutes for each four minutes of time. Now, if by progression you
are off about one year and eighteen days of pinpointing the fortunate event, you will be off four minutes of birth time. If the Moon
is applying to the Sun and you are late on the fortunate event, subtract four minutes from the birth time. If you are a year and eighteen days ahead of the event, add the four minutes to the birth time.
If the Moon is separating from the Sun, simply reverse the add-and-
subtract procedure for early or late. If you do not reverse your formula for a night birth, reverse the add-and-subtract procedure
outlined above also.

During one hour of time, Fortuna moves almost fifteen
degrees. In this same hour the Sun moves on an average of two
minutes, twenty-eight seconds. The Moon moves on an average of
thirty-three minutes. The house cusps in this same hour average
about a fifteen degree movement. Fortuna moves as fast as the
Ascendant, being a combination of all three of these chart points. If
you have plenty of time, you can be more exact by checking the
movement of the Ascendant and Fortuna. If you suspect the birth
time is off by a full hour, you will be fifteen years off on a progressed or directed hit or aspect.

My view of the various aids of sighting and/or prediction is
simply this: The natal chart is the powder keg, containing the sum
total of promises your soul came in to fulfill and work out. The
directions, progressions, solar or lunar returns are the various
agents by which the fuse is implanted in the powder keg. The transits are the match.

I've found the slower moving transiting planets to be a great
aid in adjusting hours of error. If you are using transits as your major indicator of events, you will be fifteen degrees off a hit or
aspect, per hour of error. Check backward or forward to see when
that particular planet was fifteen (or more) degrees away from your
computation of Fortuna. Adjust your birth time accordingly and re-
delineate the chart. Use fifteen degrees for hours of error. Use one
degree and three minutes for each four minutes of error and use six-
teen minutes for one minute of birth time correction.

I have found this method to be quick and satisfactory to
myself. As far as I know I am the only one to use it. It is presented

here for your consideration, amusement or whatever it evokes in you. If anyone tries it and wants to make comments on it, I would be most happy to hear from you. If anyone wants me to rectify their charts by this method, I will probably not answer because I am not in the business of chart rectification, except for my own purposes.

ALPHABETICAL BIBLIOGRAPHY
AND REFERENCE LIST

A to Z Horoscope Maker and Delineator
Llewellyn George (St. Paul: Llewellyn Publications, 1969)

Arabic Points and Human Contracts
Elizabeth Aldrich (undated, privately circulated lecture series)

An Astrological Guide to Your Sex Life
Vivian E. Robson (New York: Bell Publishing Co., 1963)

The Astrological 'Parts' and the Algebra of Life
Dane Rudhyar (*American Journal of Astrology*: Autumn, 1936)

Complete Method of Prediction
Robert deLuce (Los Angeles: DeLuce Publishing Co., 1935)

The Determination of Sex from the Horoscope and Visa Versa
Richard H. Delano (*A.F.A. Bulletin*: October, 1969)

The Elements of Astrology
Al-Biruni (London: Luzac & Co., 1934; English translation of 1029 A.D. Arabic original)

Hidden Point in the Horoscope
E.H. Bailey (undated paper)

Importance of the Part of Fortune in the Chart
Elsie Margaret Knapp (*Horoscope Magazine*: January, 1968)

The Magical Arabian Parts
Elizabeth Aldrich (*American Astrology Magazine*: January & April, 1937; December, 1938)

Occupational Parts
John Parker Vreeland (*Wynn's Astrology Magazine*: January, 1937

A 'Part of Fortune' for the Midheaven
Dane Rudhyar (*Horoscope Magazine*: November, 1972)

The Part of Fortune: Roadsign on Your Way to Success
Herschel Heineman (*American Astrological Quarterly*: Winter, 1972)

The Part of Mind
Ruth Gerry (lecture at A.F.A. Convention, Washington, DC, 1966)

The Parts of the Planets
Antoin Bois (undated, privately circulated paper)

The Point of Karma
Edith Painton (undated, privately circulated lecture series)

The Power of Purpose of the Part of Fortune
John Jocelyn (paper written early 1941 at the Aquarian College, Brooklyn, NY)

Secret Good Luck in Your Birth Chart
Nancy Langford (*Astrology Guide*: December, 1971)

Sensitive Points
Vivian E. Robson (*The British Journal of Astrology*: December, 1936—May, 1937)

Sensitive Points
Karl Prandler Pracht (*American Astrology Magazine*: January-February, 1946)

Simplified Horary Astrology
Ivy M. Goldstein-Jacobson (Alhambra, CA: Frank Severy Publishers, 1979)

The Way of Astrology
Ivy M. Goldstein-Jacobson (Pasadena, CA: Pasadena Lithographers, 1967)

Windows of the Mind
Marc Edmund Jones (*American Astrology Magazine*: December, 1942—October, 1943)

Your Division of Success
Elizabeth Aldrich (*American Astroloy Digest*, 1956)

Your Equilibrium Parts
Wynn (*Wynn's Astrology Magazine*: January, 1946)

Your Horoscope According to the Ancients
James R. Wolfe (*Astrology, Your Daily Horoscope*: June, 1970)

Your Part of Fortune
John Parker Vreeland (*Wynn's Astrology Magazine*: September-October, 1936)

Your Part of Love
John Parker Vreeland (Wynn's Astrology Magazine: November, 1936)

Your Threshold of...
Marc Edmond Jones (*American Astrology Magazine*: March-October, 1942)

1000 Aphorisms on Love and Marriage
Pandit Gopesh Kumar Ojha, LL. B. (Allahabad: Kitab Mahal Publishing Co., 1959)

    Cut out FORTUNE FINDER and laminate both sides with clear plastic to allow easy re-use. See page 56-57 of this book for further instructions.

    You can order a PRE-LAMINATED FORTUNE FINDER from Astro Computing Services, P.O. Box 16430, San Diego, CA 92116-0430 for $3 (including handling). Also, ask for our catalogue of calculating services.

Cut out FORTUNE FINDER and laminate both sides with clear plastic to allow easy re-use. See page 56-57 of this book for further instructions.

You can order a PRE-LAMINATED FORTUNE FINDER from Astro Computing Services, P.O. Box 16430, San Diego, CA 92116-0430 for $3 (including handling). Also, ask for our catalogue of calculating services.

    Cut out FORTUNE FINDER and laminate both sides with clear plastic to allow easy re-use. See page 56-57 of this book for further instructions.

    You can order a PRE-LAMINATED FORTUNE FINDER from Astro Computing Services, P.O. Box 16430, San Diego, CA 92116-0430 for $3 (including handling). Also, ask for our catalogue of calculating services.

Cut out FORTUNE FINDER and laminate both sides with clear plastic to allow easy re-use. See page 56-57 of this book for further instructions.

You can order a PRE-LAMINATED FORTUNE FINDER from Astro Computing Services, P.O. Box 16430, San Diego, CA 92116-0430 for $3 (including handling). Also, ask for our catalogue of calculating services.

Cut out FORTUNE FINDER and laminate both sides with clear plastic to allow easy re-use. See page 56-57 of this book for further instructions.

You can order a PRE-LAMINATED FORTUNE FINDER from Astro Computing Services, P.O. Box 16430, San Diego, CA 92116-0430 for $3 (including handling). Also, ask for our catalogue of calculating services.